The Celebrated Pedestrian

D1337365

The Celebrated Pedestrian

BBC BOOKS

BBC HISTORY magazine

13 5 7 9 10 8 6 4 2

Published in 2009 by BBC Books, an imprint of Ebury Publishing.
A Random House Group Company

This edition published in 2015

The Random House Group Limited Reg. No. 954009

Addresses for companies within the Random House Group can be found at:
www.randomhouse.co.uk

A CIP catalogue record for this book is available from the British Library.

ISBN 9781849909716

Penguin Random House is committed to a sustainable future
for our business, our readers and our planet. This book is
made from Forest Stewardship Council® certified paper.

Commissioning editor: Albert DePetrillo
Project editor: Laura Higginson
Designer: Robert Updegraff
Illustrations: Stacey Earley
Production: Phil Spencer

Printed and bound in Great Britain by Clays Ltd, St Ives PLC

To buy books by your favourite authors and register for offers, visit:
www.randomhouse.co.uk

CONTENTS

INTRODUCTION

Questions, questions. History is all about asking questions of the past and endeavouring to find the answers. Sometimes those answers inform us about the present, sometimes they cast new light on old mysteries, sometimes they challenge an orthodox view, and sometimes they just plain entertain us.

Presented in this volume is a selection of questions that we have answered in the pages of *BBC History Magazine* over the past few years, in our unimaginatively named yet regularly enlightening 'Question and Answer' section. Many of these questions were posed to us by our readers, while some occurred to the editorial team in the course of research into topics we were covering in the magazine, or, indeed, while we were waiting for inspiration to strike over our morning coffee.

We have a panel of historical experts waiting at the end of the phone, desperate to be released on whatever conundrum we set them. These bookish sorts spend their time delving into the less-studied recesses of the past, rooting out the hidden truffles of history in order to better answer such questions as whether the Sphinx really lost its nose to Napoleon's marksmen.

Of course, one of the joys of history is its general lack of absolutes (in contrast to its far from absolute lack of generals). Our questions don't tend to be the simple black and white sort that can be afforded simple yes or no answers, which is fortunate, as this would be a lugubriously tedious tome if that were the case. However, that does mean you might disagree with some of the answers – and you may even have a point. There's much to be debated here, and I'm sure there's table talk material aplenty to encourage that.

You're probably enjoying this on the toilet. If that's the case, you might want to bypass the list of noted figures from the past who breathed their last in the bathroom. But don't let that put you off: trivia lovers and quiz connoisseurs should find all manner of delights to divert them here, as should anyone who has an appetite for the past. The range of topics covered is eclectic, from the origins of the garden gnome industry to the repatriation of Second World War prisoners, taking in the Swedish suicide rate, Britain's last cannibal and the Olympic pedigree of the tug-of-war along the way.

And that brings us to the titular 'Celebrated Pedestrian', the pavement-pounding walking wonder that was Captain Barclay. If you dip inside this book, you'll find out all about his extraordinary foot-slogging endeavours, and the moment in 1809 for which he has become celebrated. That's just the sort of story that happily comes to light when you take a spirit of enthusiastic enquiry into the pages of the past.

So let's finish with a question. If you have a historical query yourself, what should you do? Just email historymagazine@bbc magazinesbristol.com, and if it's interesting enough, we'll set our historical hounds on the trail and print the answer in a future issue of Britain's bestselling history magazine, and possibly in the sequel to this book!

Dave Musgrove
Editor of *BBC History Magazine*, 2009

The Celebrated
Pedestrian

CHAPTER 1

LIFE AND DEATH, OR BOUDICCA AT KING'S CROSS

Was the embalmed body of an English queen once on display in Westminster Abbey?

Henry V's queen, Catherine of Valois, died in 1437 and her coffin was on display for centuries. Vergers charged a shilling to take off the lid so that visitors could view her mummified corpse. Samuel Pepys reports that he 'had the upper part of her body in my hands, and I did kiss her mouth, reflecting upon it that I did kiss a Queen, and that this was my birthday, 36 year old, that I did first kiss a Queen'. The body was removed from public view in 1776. *Nick Rennison*

How many English monarchs have been gay?

We know little about the earliest monarchs, but of those about whom rather more is known, only two were undoubtedly homosexual.

William II (Rufus), who ruled England from 1087 to 1100, was cheerfully blasphemous and had little respect for the Church, helping himself to ecclesiastical revenues. As a result, the monkish chroniclers delighted in recording gossip and rumour about the king, and 'evidence' of his homosexuality made up a large part of this. He wore his hair long and decorated with ribbons, while his shoes and clothes were thought effeminate.

The second king thought to be homosexual was Edward II, who ruled from 1307 to 1327. Edward heaped honours and wealth on his male lovers. The most famous was Piers Gaveston, whose sharp wit wounded the pride of many noblemen and earned him the enemies who would kill him in 1312. Edward later took Hugh Despenser the Younger as a favourite, indulging his taste for wealth to the extreme. He too was killed by rebellious nobles, in 1326.

There have been claims that other monarchs of the past may have been secretly homosexual, Richard I among them (see page 20). They remain unproven. *Rupert Matthews*

Who was the first person to be killed in a car accident?

On 17 August 1896 Bridget Driscoll was walking in the grounds of the Crystal Palace when she stepped into the path of a motor car giving demonstration rides to the public. Travelling at a reckless speed of 4 mph, the car caused fatal injuries, giving Mrs Driscoll the dubious distinction of being the world's first victim of the automobile. *Nick Rennison*

How did prostitutes avoid pregnancy before modern contraceptive methods?

The history of female prostitution is long and complex, and to generalise about contraception is difficult. However, it's probably best to assume that prostitutes were simply proficient users of the prevailing methods of contraception used in their particular society. Perhaps the earliest known forms were pessaries (a type of diaphragm) lubricated with honey or oil, used in ancient Egypt. There were also 'barrier' methods, such as sponges and plugs made of beeswax or oiled paper. Condoms, made of animal gut, appeared in Europe in the 17th century.

There is a tendency to believe that intercourse carried a high pregnancy risk before the contraceptive pill arrived in the 1960s. This is not necessarily true: the 19th and 20th centuries saw many advances in contraception, such as spermicidal creams and latex condoms. But of course many prostitutes did get pregnant and might well have resorted to abortion, an ancient practice involving either herbal preparations, physical intervention or exercise. Hippocrates, for instance, advised a pregnant prostitute to jump up and down a lot. Until the onset of medicalised abortion, terminations were the domain of women with a certain amount of knowledge. Some historians believe the witch-hunts of the 16th and 17th centuries were partly an attempt by a male-dominated establishment to wipe out female knowledge of contraception and abortion. *Eugene Byrne*

Is it true that there was one man who survived the sinking of both the *Titanic* and the *Lusitania*?

The story of Frank Tower, a stoker who supposedly survived the sinking of the *Titanic* in 1912 and was also rescued from the waters after a U-boat sank the *Lusitania* in 1915, has long been in circulation. The idea that there was a man lucky enough to survive both disasters is an appealing one, but sadly there is little evidence that it is true. Certainly nobody of that name appears on the crew list (or passenger list) of either ship. The tale probably began life as a sailor's yarn ('I once knew a man who…') and was repeated enough to become an urban legend. *Nick Rennison*

Did George Washington, as legend has it, really have wooden dentures?

The story that George Washington had wooden dentures made for him is often repeated, but it is only a legend. Certainly Washington had a lifelong problem with his teeth, and when he became president he had only one natural tooth left. The truth about his dentures is perhaps more surprising than the myth. He had many sets, and one in particular had the base and the upper teeth made out of walrus ivory, while the lower plate consisted of human teeth extracted from corpses. *Nick Rennison*

I came across a burial entry for 'a crisom child' in a 17th-century church register. What does it mean?

This is an unusual entry. The phrase 'crisom baby' is not a medical term but an ecclesiastical one. Strictly speaking, a crisom baby is an infant that is being christened – in much the same way that a bride is a woman being married. While the phrase properly meant a baby undergoing the church service, it was used rather loosely to describe a newly born baby that either had not yet been christened, or had only just undergone the ceremony. In this case, the baby would seem to have been buried very soon after birth. *Rupert Matthews*

What was the Great Stink?

In early Victorian London, raw sewage was regularly dumped in the Thames, and the stench could be overpowering. In 1858, the year of the Great Stink, the smell was so appalling that curtains in the House of Commons were soaked in chloride of lime in a vain attempt to protect MPs from the noxious fumes. At last, the severity of the smell prompted them into action, and an Act of Parliament was rushed through in 18 days, providing money for new sewers. *Nick Rennison*

Is it true that Boudicca is buried under Platform 10 at King's Cross?

Sadly, this is a myth. The truth is we don't know where she was buried. The story probably originated in the 1930s when a writer, Lewis Spence, claimed that the battle between Boudicca's army and the Romans took place in the valley where King's Cross Station now stands. Although he never suggested that Boudicca was buried there, the idea that she was caught people's imagination. *Nick Rennison*

Have the remains of Anne Boleyn (or her cousin Katherine Howard) ever been exhumed from the Chapel of St Peter ad Vincula and examined?

There are no records of either queen's body being exhumed. The chapel of St Peter ad Vincula (in chains) lies within the bounds of the Tower of London and is full of the bodies of the famous, many of them minus their heads. Sir Thomas More and the ill-fated Lady Jane Grey, both beheaded, are also buried there. *Nick Rennison*

Was Julius Caesar really born by Caesarean section? Is this the origin of the term?

It could be the origin of the term, but any such derivation is based on false information about Caesar's birth. In Roman times Caesarean section was only used to deliver babies from dead mothers. With no antibiotics and no anaesthetics, it would have been virtually impossible for a woman to survive such an operation anyway. Julius Caesar's mother, Aurelia Cotta, lived until her son was middle-aged, so she could not have undergone a Caesarean section. *Nick Rennison*

10 Famous people who drowned

They all met a watery end.

1 **William Adelin**
prince (son of Henry I), aboard the *White Ship*

2 **Frederick Barbarossa**
Holy Roman Emperor, fording the River Saleph, 1190

3 **George, Duke of Clarence**
conspirator, allegedly in a butt of malmsey wine, 1478

4 **Dorothy Bradford**
Mayflower passenger, fell overboard, 1620

5 **Percy Bysshe Shelley**
poet, off the Italian coast, 1822

6 **Matthew Webb**
Channel swimmer, under Niagara Falls, 1883

7 **Lord Kitchener**
soldier, aboard HMS *Hampshire*, 1916

8 **Virginia Woolf**
writer, suicide in the River Ouse, 1941

9 **Brian Jones**
musician, in his swimming pool, 1969

10 **Robert Maxwell**
publisher, fell from his yacht, 1991

Did you know…?

Alexander, King of Greece from 1917 to 1920, died from blood poisoning at the age of 27 after he was attacked and bitten by two monkeys while walking in the Royal Gardens in Athens.
Nick Rennison

Was Oliver Cromwell Welsh?

Cromwell's great-grandfather was called Morgan Williams, and he was one of a Welsh family, originally from Glamorgan but living in London at the end of the 15th century. Williams married the older sister of Thomas Cromwell, later to be Henry VIII's chief minister, in 1497. Morgan Williams's sons began to call themselves Cromwell in honour of their mother's famous brother. So, in a sense, one of the most archetypal of Englishmen was, at least in his origins, part Welsh. *Nick Rennison*

Is it true that Stalin's purges were driven by grief as a result of his wife's death?

Stalin's second wife, Nadya Alliluyeva, shot a bullet through her heart in 1932, plunging her husband into grief. Alternating between guilt, anger and sorrow, the Soviet premier was deeply shaken by what had happened, and for a while his aides feared he might follow a similar course. Nadya's death might well have had a permanent effect on his personality. His close colleague Lazar Kaganovich observed that 'after 1932, Stalin changed'. Over a million people died in the great purges of the mid- to late 1930s, and it is not inconceivable that Stalin's personal tragedy dimmed his sympathies for the misfortunes of others. His nephew claimed that it 'made the Terror inevitable'. However, the purges were also caused by a number of external factors hardly connected to Nadya, and Stalin already had a long history of using violence to get his way. During the civil war, over a decade earlier, he ordered hundreds of shootings, and is reputed to have said 'death solves all problems'.

Stalin's first wife, Ekaterina Svanidze, also died tragically, of tuberculosis, in 1907. The young widower told a friend 'with her have died my last warm feelings for people'. This event too has been proffered as the reason for the Stalinist excesses, but the real story is probably more complex. *Rob Attar*

I have read that in early modern England the age of first marriage for men and women was later than in the Victorian era. Why was this?

There is clear evidence that in Britain the average age of first marriage dropped in the later 18th century. From an average of roughly 25, the average age dropped to around 22 by the early 19th century. Explanations for this drop focus on the agricultural and industrial revolutions. In a nation of rural villages, aristocratic households and small towns, there were powerful family, social and economic pressures against impulsive early marriages. But improving diet, more secure food supplies, increasing prosperity and a wider choice of job opportunities might have led people to feel more optimistic about marrying sooner. Probably more important, though, is increased geographic mobility and migration to towns and cities. Young people moving away from the watchful eye of community and extended family would be more likely to marry quickly. Some research suggests that the statistics are skewed by a sizeable minority of urban working-class men and women marrying much younger, while the rest of the population actually carried on much as before. Males of the growing middle classes, for instance, tended to wait until they had established themselves in a career before marrying, a practice lasting well into the 20th century; but then they often married women considerably younger than themselves. *Eugene Byrne*

In articles about the real or imagined evils of cannabis, we're constantly told that Queen Victoria used to smoke it. True or false?

If she did take it, she certainly didn't smoke it. Although it's an axiom of pro-pot propaganda that Her Majesty took cannabis, the truth is that we don't know for sure. What we do know is that Sir John Russell Reynolds, one of her doctors in later life, devoted much of his career to studying the stuff, which was legally available from pharmacists at the time. In an 1890 article for *The Lancet*, Reynolds said that he had been prescribing *Cannabis indica*, which had been introduced from India earlier that century, for 30 years to relieve a very wide range of ailments. He described it as 'one of the most valuable medicines we possess'. It was, among other things, a 'most valuable medicine in nocturnal cramps of old and gouty people', and he also recommended it for 'senile insomnia'. Whether he had the queen in mind when he wrote this, we'll never know because there was no way a respectable doctor would break patient confidentiality. The balance of probability is that she did take it, probably in tincture form, for the pains of old age. It is also possible that she took it earlier on for menstrual cramps, but no proof exists. *Eugene Byrne*

Scholars aside, when did the population first know what year they were living in?

Throughout history people have used quite different methods to identify a particular year. The earliest method was probably to pinpoint a dramatic event, such as a major flood, and identify a year as 'three years after the flood that destroyed such and such a place'. Once writing was widespread, years were often identified by reference to the ruler. The Romans dated years by stating which two men held the supreme government office of consul. Given that whenever a consul went anywhere he was preceded by 12 men carrying axes, it is likely that most Romans would have known who was consul, and thus in which year they were living.

In Britain today we generally use the Christian method of counting years, which begins with the year in which Jesus Christ was born. For a time a rival system existed that counted from the date of Christ's crucifixion. However, by the time the Venerable Bede was writing his famous *Ecclesiastical History of the English People* in about 731, most Western scholars had accepted our

10 People killed in riding accidents

They tamed kingdoms, but their mounts were a different matter.

1 **William the Conqueror**
from internal injuries from the pommel of his saddle, 1087

2 **Fulk, King of Jerusalem**
skull crushed by his saddle, 1143

3 **Geoffrey Plantagenet**
trampled to death in a tournament, 1186

4 **Leopold V of Austria**
fell during a tournament, 1194

5 **Genghis Khan**
fell while hunting, 1227

6 **Bishop Walter de Merton**
fell while fording a river, 1277

7 **Alexander III of Scotland**
fell from his horse in a storm, 1286

8 **Marjorie, daughter of Robert Bruce**
after a fall brought on premature labour, 1316

9 **Pope Urban VI**
fell off a mule, 1389

10 **William III**
after his horse tripped on a molehill, 1702

present system. It is uncertain if the illiterate bulk of the population was aware of this system by this date. However, the end of the first millennium produced a wave of panics and apocalyptic prophecies. Quite clearly, the vast majority of the population knew that the year 1000 was approaching. It was probably somewhere between the time of Bede and this date that most people in Christendom became aware of the year in which they lived. *Rupert Matthews*

Was Richard the Lionheart a homosexual?

Although now firmly embedded in the popular imagination, the idea that Richard I was homosexual was only first broached in 1948, when John Harvey broke what he alleged to be a conspiracy of silence that had lasted for over 700 years. Besides the fact that Richard fathered no children by his queen, there are key pieces of evidence in the case, all supplied by the English chronicler Roger of Howden. In 1187 Richard is said to have shared the same bed as King Philip of France. At Messina in 1190, on his way to a crusade, he stripped naked to do public penance for his (unspecified) sins, and on his return, *c.*1195, having been warned by a hermit to amend his lifestyle and thus avoid the fate of the city of Sodom, he once again did penance, so we are told, returning to the bed of his wife from which he is assumed to have strayed. From this, various modern historians have fashioned an image of Richard as an openly 'gay' or bisexual man.

There are, however, problems with this interpretation. None of Richard's enemies accused him of deviant sexual practices, as they would have done had his homosexuality been widely known. In 1182 it was for his kidnap and alleged rape of the women, not the men, of Aquitaine that he was criticised by Roger of Howden, and he undoubtedly fathered at least one child in southern France. Sharing a bed was a political, not a sexual, gesture, and it may have been the punishment, not the crimes of Sodom, that inspired the hermit's outburst. Public penance would have been appropriate for any aspirant crusader such as Richard, keen to earn divine favour, and tells us nothing of the particular nature of the sins confessed. For these reasons, Richard's principal modern biographer, John Gillingham, utterly rejects the legend of the gay Richard. *Nicholas Vincent*

10 People who died on their birthdays

Many happy returns? Not in these cases...

1 **Elizabeth of York**
wife of Henry VII, 11 February 1503

2 **Raphael**
painter, 6 April 1520

3 **Etienne Dolet**
scholar and heretic, 3 August 1546

4 **Henry I of Portugal**
king, 31 January 1580

5 **St Lawrence of Brindisi**
diplomat and general, 22 July 1619

6 **Sir Thomas Browne**
philosopher, 19 October 1682

7 **Hugo Junkers**
aircraft designer, 3 February 1935

8 **George 'Machine-Gun' Kelly**
gangster, 18 July 1954

9 **Ingrid Bergman**
actress, 29 August 1982

10 **Henry 'Bunny' Austin**
tennis player, 26 August 2000

Who was the first British person that we know of by name?

Writing in the 12th century, the Welsh scholar Geoffrey of
Monmouth produced a *History of the Kings of Britain*, which he
claimed was based on older and largely forgotten chronicles and
histories. It is generally thought that Geoffrey simply made up the
earlier chapters of the history. According to these spurious stories,
the first humans to reach Britain were a group of Trojans who were
on the run after the sack of Troy, led by a king named Brutus. His
three sons – Albanact, Camber and Locrine – were supposedly the
first native-born Britons. Following Geoffrey of Monmouth's
chronology, they would have been born in about 1100 BC.

Of rather more certain historic reality are Julius Caesar's accounts
of Britain in 55 BC. These name two kings, Commius of the
Atrebates in what is now Sussex, and Cassivellaunus of the
Catuvellauni in modern Hertfordshire. Coins minted before the
Roman invasion of Claudius in AD 43 name a few kings, such as
Dubnovellaunos of the Cantii, Addedomaros of the Trinovantes and
Aunast (probably a contraction of a longer name) of the Coritani.
Firm dates cannot be ascribed to any of these coins, but they do seem
to have been minted after Julius Caesar's raids in 54/55 BC. On
present evidence it is likely that Commius was the earliest of the few
pre-Roman British figures who are known by name. *Rupert Matthews*

Katherine of Aragon and Anne Boleyn both suffered a number of miscarriages. Could this have been due to Henry VIII having had a balanced translocation of his chromosomes?

In a balanced translocation of chromosomes, an individual's cells divide to create egg or sperm cells for reproduction and these can have extra – or missing – genetic material that sometimes leads to miscarriage.

Katherine of Aragon had at least six pregnancies during the period 1509–18: a daughter was stillborn on 31 January 1510; Henry, Prince of Wales, died after 52 days in 1511; another son, also called Henry, lived for a few hours after his birth in November 1513; two boys and a girl – all stillbirths – followed in 1515, 1517 and 1518. Only Mary, born in February 1516, survived.

Anne Boleyn safely delivered Elizabeth in September 1533, but miscarried in 1534, and again in January 1536 (losing a heavy male foetus aged about three and a half months) after her uncle, the third Duke of Norfolk, blurted out news of Henry VIII's jousting accident five days earlier. It signalled her downfall as queen.

After nearly five centuries and without medical evidence, no firm conclusion is possible about Henry having chromosome translocation. About one person in 500 has it, but this does not necessarily cause a miscarriage or mean that healthy children

10 People who died in Venice

Historical figures who drew their last breath in Italy's city of canals, palaces and gondolas.

1 **Marco Polo**
traveller, 1324

2 **Thomas, Duke of Norfolk**
exile, 1399

3 **Titian**
painter, 1576

4 **Claudio Monteverdi**
composer, 1643

5 **Francesco Guardi**
painter, 1793

6 **Christian Doppler**
mathematician and physicist, 1853

7 **Richard Wagner**
composer, 1883

8 **Robert Browning**
poet, 1889

9 **Ezra Pound**
poet, 1972

10 **Peggy Guggenheim**
art collector, 1979

cannot be produced. Miscarriages also occur through viral infection and nutritional imbalance, which, given the primitive hygiene and unhealthy diet of Tudor times, look the more likely reasons. *Listeria monocytogenes*, a bacterium found in stream water and food, causes listeriosis, which triggers spontaneous abortion or stillbirth. This also manifests itself as meningitis or pneumonia in newborns, which may have killed the two boys that Katherine safely delivered. It can also involve septicaemia, which probably caused Jane Seymour's death in October 1537, 12 days after she gave birth to a healthy son, who was to become Edward VI. Pregnant women are nowadays advised not to eat certain foods, such as unpasteurised cheese, because of the danger of contracting listeria. In fact, after Jane's death, Henry's minister Thomas Cromwell blamed her attendants for allowing her to eat the wrong kinds of food 'as her fantasy in sickness called for' or letting her catch cold. *Robert Hutchinson*

Back in the 1960s and 1970s it was commonly believed that Sweden, despite its high standard of living, had the highest suicide rate in the world. Yet this turns out not to be true. How did this idea of suicidal Swedes arise?

Sweden's suicide rate is moderate to high in global terms, but distinctly average by developed world standards. Since the 1950s (as far back as the statistics for the most advanced economies go), it's generally been higher than those of Britain and the Netherlands, lower than that of Denmark, and very roughly comparable to France. However, the Swedes never, ever topped the league.

Comparing statistics across cultures is difficult. Religious or cultural conditions play a part in suicide rates, and the reporting of them. In the past, doctors and coroners in some countries would ascribe a suicide to another cause to protect relatives from stigma – on anecdotal evidence, this was widespread in Victorian Britain. Other cultures see suicide as a sometimes honourable course of action, which is why Japan is close to the top of the table.

It was once thought that Sweden's supposedly high number of suicides was simply because their doctors were more honest. However, most Swedes blame US President Eisenhower, who at a

Republican Party function in 1960 claimed that 'a fairly friendly European country' – everyone understood him to mean Sweden – suffered from lack of ambition, drunkenness and a soaring suicide rate as a result of the 'socialistic' policies of its government. Swedish suicide rates at that time had not increased at all. In fact, at the height of the cold war this neutral country with a sophisticated welfare system, successful economy and high standard of living was looked on with envy by many Europeans, but as a threat by right-wing Americans. Eisenhower might have launched a myth that everyone swallowed after thinking of endless winter nights and watching Ingmar Bergman movies. *Eugene Byrne*

What's the earliest record we have of someone dying of a smoking-related disease?

Tobacco was consumed in Native American societies perhaps 2000 years ago, but the conventional wisdom is that its use was occasional and ceremonial or medicinal, so it might not have had the damaging effects we associate with it nowadays.

When Europeans started to use it, some people, at least, considered it harmful. Long before Professor Richard Doll's findings in the 1950s and 1960s linking smoking to lung cancer, James I's famous *Counterblaste to Tobacco* (1604) said smoking was 'dangerous to the lungs'. But many 17th- and 18th-century medical authorities who claimed tobacco was harmful focused on cancers of the nose, mouth and throat. This was probably because consuming tobacco in pipes or as snuff was more likely to trigger these diseases; lung cancer was very rare until the advent of the cigarette in the mid-19th century.

It's generally claimed that the first documented Briton killed by tobacco was Sir Thomas Harriot (1560–1621). He was one of Sir Walter Raleigh's circle, and had travelled to Virginia in 1585–6. He and Raleigh pioneered pipe smoking in England, and Harriot's heavy consumption is the likely cause of the cancerous tumour of the nose that killed him. In truth, however, there may be earlier claimants to the dubious honour of Europe's first tobacco fatality, particularly in Spain, where it had arrived some decades sooner. *Eugene Byrne*

10 People said to have suffered from syphillis

The so-called 'French disease' was no respecter of nationality.

1 **John Keats**
(1795–1821) English poet

2 **Franz Schubert**
(1797–1828) Austrian composer

3 **Abraham Lincoln**
(1809–65) American president

4 **Robert Schumann**
(1810–56) German composer

5 **Charles Baudelaire**
(1821–67) French poet

6 **Gustave Flaubert**
(1821–80) French writer

7 **Paul Gauguin**
(1848–1903) French artist

8 **Lord Randolph Churchill**
(1849–95) English statesman

9 **Guy de Maupassant**
(1850–93) French writer

10 **Al Capone**
(1899–1947) American gangster

In the BBC series The Tudors, Cardinal Wolsey was shown committing suicide by cutting his throat. Is this historically correct?

Cardinal Thomas Wolsey (c.1470–1530) was Lord Chancellor during the early part of King Henry VIII's reign. He ran many aspects of the kingdom's government for over 14 years. As a cardinal and Archbishop of York, Wolsey was also a leading figure in the Church hierarchy. He fell from power when he failed to persuade the pope to annul Henry's marriage to Catherine of Aragon. When Wolsey's enemies showed Henry evidence that his Lord Chancellor had been conducting inappropriate secret diplomacy, the king ordered Wolsey to be arrested for treason and brought to London for trial. On the journey south, Wolsey died at Leicester Abbey. The only contemporary writer who hints at suicide was Edward Hall, who recorded 'men said he willingly took so much strong purgative [laxative] that his constitution could not bear it. But Sir William Kingston comforted him, and by easy journeys he brought him to the Abbey of Leicester on 27 November, where through weakness caused by purgatives and vomiting he died the second night following, and is buried in the same Abbey'. Other sources say merely that Wolsey fell ill, and

10 People said to have died in the bathroom

Will you be much longer in there?

1 **Seneca the Younger**
statesman, committed suicide
in the bath, AD 65

2 **Commodus**
Roman emperor, strangled by
a wrestler, AD 192

3 **Elagabalus**
Roman emperor, killed by his
soldiers in the latrine, AD 222

4 **Edmund Ironside**
King of England, stabbed in the
bowels while relieving himself,
1016

5 **Arthur Capell**
Earl of Essex, cut his own throat
while on his close-stool in the
Tower, 1683

6 **George II**
King of England, died of
heart failure on the toilet,
1760

7 **Jean-Paul Marat**
French revolutionary, stabbed
in his bath by Charlotte Corday,
1793

8 **Catherine the Great**
Tsarina of Russia, died of a
stroke, 1796

9 **Judy Garland**
actress, died of an overdose,
1969

10 **Jim Morrison**
musician, overdosed in his
Paris home, 1971

even Hall introduced his account with the words 'men said', indicating that he was merely passing on rumour, not established fact. The most likely scenario is that Wolsey died a natural death. He most certainly did not slit his throat. *Rupert Matthews*

If workmen on a building site were to uncover the grave of some victim(s) of the Black Death or Great Plague, what would happen?

Burial sites are quite commonly unearthed by building work in older parts of old towns and cities, and there are strict procedures for dealing with them. If human remains are found, work has to stop immediately and the police must be called in case the death is recent and suspicious. If the remains are historic, the dead will be reburied. Only in cases of strong historic or scientific interest are remains exhumed for examination.

The local environmental health department is also called in because so many of our ancestors were carried off by infectious disease. Where smallpox or anthrax were concerned there is a very slight danger that infectious agents remain. During plague pandemics the dead were often buried en masse in pits. The Public Health Laboratory Service says: 'Plague pits present no hazards... The organisms that caused mass deaths in the past do not survive well outside living hosts and are unlikely to withstand the intense microbial competition that occurs in decay.' Coffins, especially lead or lead-lined ones, are treated with more care as they often preserve partially mummified bodies, soft tissue and/or black goo known as 'coffin liquor'. These are handled by environmental health staff in protective gear. There are no known cases of anyone catching the plague from the remains of its earlier victims.
Eugene Byrne

10 People blind in one eye

What caused these historical figures to lose their sight in one eye?

1 **Hannibal**
(247–182 BC) Punic leader; infection

2 **Xiahou Dun**
(died AD 220) Chinese general; stray arrow

3 **Jan Zizka**
(1360–1424) Hussite soldier; childhood fight

4 **Horatio Nelson**
(1758–1805) British admiral; debris from cannon shot

5 **André Massena**
(1758–1817) French marshal; accidentally shot, probably by Napoleon

6 **Elizabeth Blackwell**
(1821–1910) first US female doctor; infection

7 **Theodore Roosevelt**
(1858–1919) US president; boxing injury

8 **Moshe Dayan**
(1915–81) Israeli military leader; sniper's bullet

9 **Sammy Davis Jr**
(1925–90) American singer; car crash

10 **Gordon Brown**
(born 1951) British politician; rugby injury

Did any Victorian matrons ever really cover up piano legs for fear they might cause sexual arousal among the menfolk?

This cliché about supposed Victorian prudery is an absurd libel on a society where, for instance, women's fashions frequently exposed shoulders and cleavage, and we cannot find a single historian who ever took the idea seriously. The likely origin of the story does tell us something interesting, though. It appears to be a tale of British anti-Americanism. In 1839 the naval hero and author Captain Frederick Marryat published *A Diary in America, with Remarks on its Institutions*. Marryat poked a lot of fun at the provincialism and prudery of the colonials, claiming that even the word 'leg' was considered indelicate. He added that he'd visited a girls' school where the legs of a piano had been dressed by the headmistress 'in modest little trousers, with frills at the bottom of them'. Marryat was supposedly burnt in effigy in the USA after his book was published, while some Americans alleged the whole story had been told to Marryat by John van Buren (son of the president) to see if he'd be gullible enough to publish it.

What had started out as a poke at Americans seems to have morphed down the years into a 'fact' about British Victorians. What is certainly true is that many pianos on both sides of the Atlantic did have covered legs – to protect them from cat claws, dogs, brooms and the kicking feet of small children enduring hours of having to practise scales. *Eugene Byrne*

Why was Joan of Arc so called when she actually came from the village of Domrémy?

The word 'Arc' is not a reference to a place name. 'Of Arc' is an English translation of the French *d'Arc*, which was what became the accepted approximation of Joan's family name. Since apostrophes were not used in names at the time, the likelihood is that her father's name was simply 'Darc'. In her own surviving signatures she appears only as 'Jehanne'. It's all very complicated and it might be easier just to call her the Maid of Orleans. *Nick Rennison*

CHAPTER 2

LANGUAGE, OR THE ORIGINAL NOSY PARKER

Who was the original Nosy Parker?

The term is often supposed to derive from a 16th-century Archbishop of Canterbury, Matthew Parker, who took a detailed interest in the lives of his clergy. However, nobody was described as a 'nosy parker' until centuries after Matthew Parker's death. One explanation is that the phrase comes from park-keepers or 'parkers' employed to patrol Hyde Park in the 19th century and make sure that lovers didn't get too amorous in the bushes. Or it could perhaps originate from the term 'nose-poker'? *Nick Rennison*

Is it true that the word 'hoodwink' derives from falconry?

The verb 'to hoodwink', meaning originally 'to blindfold', dates back to the 16th century and was used by Shakespeare in *Romeo and Juliet*. It may derive from the practice of hooding falcons until they were ready to strike at their prey, but it is just as likely to be a literal reference to covering someone's eyes with a hood. *Nick Rennison*

Why are heroes in historical fiction 'swashbuckling'? What does it mean?

A 'buckler' was a type of small shield, and the verb 'to swash' meant to race about, brandishing your sword in mock fights. In the 16th century a swashbuckler was someone who disturbed the peace with noisy and drunken threats of violence, a kind of Tudor lager lout. Over the centuries it came to mean a more dashing and romantic swordsman. *Nick Rennison*

As 'septem' is the Latin word for 'seven', why is September the ninth month in the calendar rather than the seventh?

For much of Roman history, the New Year was deemed to begin on 1 March, so September was the seventh month. The months of January and February were added around the 8th century BC, but they were not placed at the beginning of the calendar until 153 BC, when the Roman consuls, after whom the years were named, started being chosen on 1 January. At this point September was shuffled back to ninth place. The name, however, was retained and continues to be used today. *Nick Rennison*

Speaking the 'Queen's English' as we do today, how far back in history could we go and still be understood?

All languages change over time, and English is no exception. But those changes are neither smooth nor gradual. One significant change in English came with the so-called Great Vowel Shift. This took place quite quickly between about 1390 and 1420, though some changes took longer. Basically, the pronunciation of English was revolutionised as people began pronouncing the vowels within words in a very different way. The causes of the Great Vowel Shift are contentious, but were probably linked both to sociological changes then taking place and to the abandonment of French as the language

10 People who stammered

Historical figures who didn't let their speech impediment hold them back.

1 **Claudius**
   (10 BC–AD 54) emperor

2 **Louis II**
   (846–879) King of France

3 **Charles Lamb**
   (1775–1834) essayist

4 **Charles Kingsley**
   (1819–75) novelist

5 **Charles Dodgson (Lewis Carroll)**
   (1832–98) author/academic

6 **William Somerset Maugham**
   (1874–1965) author and playwright

7 **George VI**
   (1895–52) King of Britain

8 **Aneurin Bevan**
   (1897–1960) politician

9 **Kim Philby**
   (1912–88) traitor

10 **Marilyn Monroe**
   (1926–62) screen idol

at court. During the Great Vowel Shift most vowels got shorter. The word 'mouse', for instance, had previously been pronounced more like 'moose', and the word 'make' more like 'mark'.

Beginning rather earlier than the Great Vowel Shift and taking longer to complete was a dramatic change in grammar. Before about 1100 English was an inflected language, with the ending of words varying, as does modern German or ancient Latin. By about 1400 inflexion had been replaced by word order as the main grammatical tool.

Taken together, the Great Vowel Shift and the loss of inflexion means that a modern native English speaker could probably, with a little practice, understand the language spoken in around 1450, would have trouble with English spoken around 1400, and would seriously struggle to understand the spoken word around 1300. Before that date a translator would be needed. *Rupert Matthews*

What is the meaning of the word 'holocaust'?

It comes from the Greek *holokauston*, meaning a 'completely (*holos*) burnt (*kaustos*)' sacrificial offering, and was originally used in the Bible. Its conventional current use – in reference to the genocide of Jews during the Second World War – was first recorded in 1942, though its popularisation dates from the late 1950s and is sometimes associated with the writer and Auschwitz survivor, Elie Wiesel. Earlier usage of the word 'holocaust' (in the non-religious context), describing natural disasters or the death of large numbers of people, dates back to the mid-19th century. The First World War, for instance, was habitually referred to as a holocaust during the inter-war years, and Winston Churchill used the word in 1929 in reference to the Armenian genocide that began in 1915. It is worth noting that post-war usage of 'holocaust' has not been restricted to the Jewish sense. During the cold war, for example, the word was commonly used in connection with the prospect of mass destruction in a nuclear war. In recent years, however, the word has increasingly been used exclusively in reference to the Nazi Judeocide. It is now conventional that when capitalised, 'Holocaust' refers to that genocide, while in lower case the word still retains its broader original meaning. *Roger Moorhouse*

WILLIAM the BASTARD

What qualifies a monarch to get the appellation 'the Great'? Why is Good Queen Bess not known as Elizabeth the Great?

Well-known titles, such as Alfred the Great, tend to be the work of chroniclers and poets. Many are given long after the king or queen in question is dead, when more is known about their work and new monarchs are held in comparison. Titles often reflect the sympathies and affections of the people, rather than any political judgement.

Some titles are, of course, more sympathetic than others. Charles the Bold (the Burgundian brother-in-law of Edward IV) would certainly have enjoyed his. Other monarchs – such as Charles the Simple (the 10th-century king of France), William the Bastard of Normandy, and Bloody Mary – would not have regarded theirs with a lot of affection. Why not Elizabeth the Great? Was she indeed as great as modern-day publishing suggests? Her reign was certainly a golden age, but the fact is that after her death in 1603, most monarchs had to make do with constitutional titles. None of the Stuarts and most certainly no Hanoverian deserved, or had, a nickname. Perhaps historians should suggest them for James I, Charles I and II, William III and Mary Stuart, Anne, Georges I–IV, William IV, Victoria, Edward VII, Edward VIII, George VI and, of course, Elizabeth II. *Christopher Lee*

Where did the phrase 'namby-pamby' originate?

It comes from a mocking reference to an 18th-century poet called Ambrose Phillips, who wrote some twee children's verses. Another writer, Henry Carey, ridiculed them as 'Namby-Pamby's Little Rhymes', taking the first syllable of Phillips's Christian name and making a silly nickname out of it. The name was soon applied to other people as well as the unfortunate Phillips. *Nick Rennison*

Why is the flag of a pirate ship traditionally called the 'Jolly Roger'?

'Jolly Roger' is probably a corruption of the French words *jolie rouge* (pretty red), which were applied originally to the red flags of French privateers. Other derivations have been suggested, including the possibility of a connection with the phrase 'Old Roger', meaning the Devil, but the French origin is most likely. *Nick Rennison*

Why are 'Darby and Joan' clubs so called? Who were they?

The names Darby and Joan for a devoted old couple date back to a ballad by Henry Woodfall, published in 1735. Woodfall's son was apprenticed to a man called John Darby, and Woodfall senior might have chosen to commemorate his son's elderly master and wife in his verse. *Nick Rennison*

What evidence have we got for the British tribes such as the Iceni, Atrebates and Belgae speaking a 'Celtic tongue'?

The tribes that inhabited Britain before the invasion of the Romans in the first century AD were a diverse and mixed group of proudly independent peoples. They did, however, share a great deal in the way of culture, religion and language – with each other and with tribes on the European continent. The evidence for this comes from a number of sources. Roman writers explicitly state that the peoples of Britain spoke languages similar to those of tribes on the Continent west of the Rhine. The Romans called these peoples Gauls, the word 'Celt' being derived from the Greek term for peoples with a similar culture who lived in the Danube basin. There is also evidence from place names and personal names to indicate that the people of Britain spoke languages similar to those of the Gauls in Europe. Exactly what these ancient languages were like it is impossible to reconstruct. We cannot be certain how similar the language of the Iceni was to that of the Atrebates, or indeed to that of the Parisii in Gaul. It is possible, however, to trace the descent of these languages through various medieval forms to modern Welsh, Gaelic, Cornish and Manx. The term 'Celtic' wasn't used to describe these modern languages until the 18th century, when scholars began to recognise their links with the ancient tongues of Britain.
Rupert Matthews

Blue Peter is a children's programme on BBC TV. It is also the name of a Battle of Britain Memorial Flight Hurricane and a pub in the West Country. So who (or what) exactly was Blue Peter?

It's a maritime signal flag, which originated in the late 18th-century Royal Navy. It's blue with a white square in the middle and signals the letter P. It was also used in port to summon all hands and passengers aboard, usually hoisted 24 hours before a ship was due to depart.

The children's TV programme takes its name from the flag. The programme was devised in the late 1950s by producer John Hunter Blair, who used the name to imply that his young viewers were to be taken on a voyage of adventure and discovery. This then inspired the choice of theme tune, a sea

10 Notable French eponymists

These people lent their names to things good and bad.

1 **Jean Nicot**
   (1530–1600) diplomat and
   tobacco importer: nicotine

2 **François Mansart**
   (1598–1666) architect:
   mansard roof

3 **Jean Martinet**
   (died 1672) military
   disciplinarian: martinet

4 **Pierre Magnol**
   (1638–1715) botanist:
   magnolia

5 **Etienne de Silhouette**
   (1709–67) parsimonious
   financier: silhouette

6 **Joseph-Ignace Guillotin**
   (1738–1814) advocate of 'humane'
   executions: guillotine

7 **Alphonse de Sade**
   (1740–1814) writer:
   sadism

8 **Nicholas Chauvin**
   (born c.1780) legendary soldier and
   Bonapartist: chauvinism

9 **Louis Pasteur**
   (1822–95) chemist:
   pasteurisation

10 **Jules Léotard**
   (c.1842–70) acrobat and
   trapeze artist: leotard

shanty called 'Barnacle Bill'. The famous sailing ship logo is from a design by artist Tony Hart, one of the programme's regular guests in its early days.

We know of two Blue Peter pubs in the United Kingdom, one in Polperro, Cornwall, presumably named after some seafaring connection. There's also a Blue Peter in Derby, miles from any sea, which was one of three identical pubs opened there in the 1930s, all with 'Blue' in their names – the others being the Blue Pool and the Blue Boy.

There was also a very famous racehorse named Blue Peter, who won both the Derby and the 2000 Guineas in 1939. The Battle of Britain Memorial Flight's *Blue Peter* is a Spitfire (not a Hurricane) and is painted in the livery of the aircraft flown by Squadron Leader George Denholm, who named his aeroplane in honour of this speedy thoroughbred. *Eugene Byrne*

What is the historical origin of the term 'slush fund'?

Although not immediately recognisable as such, 'slush fund' is one of the many words and phrases in the English language that derive from nautical terms. 'Slush' was the fat left over after the boiling of salted meat, the staple food of seamen during the age of sail. It was often sold on to candle-makers and soap manufacturers and the money put into a 'slush fund' used to buy small luxuries for the sailors. *Nick Rennison*

I've heard that the phrase 'on your tod' somehow refers to a jockey in the Edwardian era. Can this story possibly be true? And if so, how?

Born in America in 1874, James 'Todhunter' Sloan was a jockey who arrived in Britain in 1896, and the following year rode for the then Prince of Wales, later Edward VII. A brilliant rider who won many races, he was forever in the newspapers, and became a popular figure with the London working class, but later fell into bad ways and died impoverished and alone. 'On your Tod Sloan' was adopted as rhyming slang for 'on your own', and then usually abbreviated to 'on your tod'. *Nick Rennison*

What was the original meaning and context of appeasement, and why has it become such a 'dirty' word?

In its original meaning 'appeasement' was an entirely honourable concept, i.e. the peaceful settlement of disputes through negotiation and compromise. In this it was in tune with the spirit of the age, as many believed that the slaughter of the First World War should be followed by a new era of multilateralism and conciliation.

With regard to Germany, appeasement was also commonly seen as the appropriate response to Nazi aggression and expansionist designs. First, Nazi Germany was anti-Communist, and communism was widely viewed as a greater threat to the established order than fascism. But, most importantly, there was also a widespread feeling that Germany had been harshly treated after the First World War, and that some accommodation of German grievances – and some negotiated territorial concessions – would be necessary to make the peace of 1919 more workable and to leave Germany pacified and quiescent. The problem with this high-minded principle was that the Nazis were determined not to be pacified, and indeed exploited appeasement – which they viewed as weakness – for all they could get, consistently ramping up their demands and refusing to compromise. As Hitler confided to a deputy, 'We must always demand so much that we can never be satisfied.' Appeasement, therefore, not only failed to prevent the Second World War, it was even considered to have contributed to its outbreak. For this reason, appeasement was thoroughly discredited and has since come to be equated, unfairly perhaps, with cowardice, a lack of scruples and the craven surrender to aggression. *Roger Moorhouse*

Reading a book on Roman Britain, I was surprised to learn that the early history of the British and Celtic tribes came mainly from Roman scholars. Does this mean no written documents from that time survive in their own languages?

The Roman invasion of Britain and other parts of northern Europe was a clash of cultures every bit as profound as it was a clash of armies. Nowhere was this made clearer than in the attitude of the two systems to record-keeping. Roman society and government relied upon the written word. Financial accounts, government records and personal information were all kept in written form in great detail. Not much survived the fall of Rome, though a few books were preserved. At this point the indigenous Britons did not yet write in their own languages, and the only surviving documents relating to them are in Latin. They had a different but no less sophisticated system of record-keeping based on the oral word. Men were trained to remember things, and often did so in verse form. Agreements and treaties were made verbally and sworn to in front of witnesses. Histories were remembered as epic poetry and songs. None of this was of interest to the Roman bureaucracy, so none of it was written down. It was not until centuries after the fall of Rome that Christian monks began to write anything in any language other than Latin or Greek. The earliest written forms of a British Celtic language are short pieces of old Welsh dating from about AD 650, preserved in books dating from around 900.
Rupert Matthews

Why was the empire called 'Roman' when the language its citizens spoke was 'Latin'?

The Roman Empire was centred on the city of Rome, but originally the Romans were only one of a number of peoples living on the plain of Latium in central Italy. These 'Latini' spoke the language known as Latin. As the Romans gradually made themselves masters of Italy, Latin established itself as the predominant literary and spoken language throughout the country, and later throughout the empire. *Nick Rennison*

Is there a historical reason why we talk about people being 'sent to Coventry'?

It is usually assumed that the phrase dates from the English Civil War (1642–9), when groups of Royalist prisoners sent to the strongly Parliamentarian city of Coventry were shunned by the locals. Being 'sent to Coventry' came to mean 'being ostracised'. However, the first recorded use of the phrase dates from nearly a century later, so it is difficult to prove the connection with the Civil War. *Nick Rennison*

CHAPTER 3

ART AND ARCHITECTURE, OR THE REAL MRS GRUNDY

Why does Chesterfield church have a crooked spire?

Although the spire on Chesterfield's St Mary and All Saints Parish Church is indeed crooked – it leans more than 3 metres (9 feet) from its true centre – it started its life straight. It was completed around 1400, but comments about its unusual appearance began only in the late 18th century. Various legends have sprung up to explain its decline. One says that the Devil knocked it with his tail as he fled a blacksmith who had hammered a nail into his foot. The local favourite is that the spire was so amazed when a virgin was married in its church that it twisted itself round to get a better look.

However, the likely truth is far more prosaic, and it comes down to slap-dash medieval building techniques. The spire was made of green timber, which moves unpredictably when it dries; there's also very little cross-bracing, so only a few timbers would need to move or rot for the whole structure to be affected. *Steph Gapper*

Who was the first person to argue that Shakespeare did not write the plays attributed to him?

In the 18th century several writers suggested that the plays were not written by Shakespeare, but an eccentric American writer and teacher called Delia Bacon was the first person to publish a major book, in 1857, devoted to the theory that the plays were the work of several others – among them someone who shared her family name, Francis Bacon. *Nick Rennison*

Prior to Gutenberg's invention of printing with movable type, did any printing at all exist?

Johannes Gutenberg printed the first complete book using movable type – a Bible – in 1455. This book was printed in Mainz and 48 copies survive. However, he and others had been developing the skills of printing for some years before. Gutenberg is thought to have begun printing around 1439, using solid blocks of type and illustrations, as were Johann Fust, Peter Schöffer and Laurens Janszoon, among others. Fragments of a Latin Grammar dating to before 1451 appear to have been printed using movable type, at least in part.

The techniques of printing had reached Europe from Asia some years earlier. The oldest known printed work in Asia states that it was printed on 11 May 868. This is a 5-metre (16-foot) scroll made up of seven block-printed panels of sayings of the Buddha. These became fairly common in Asia over the following centuries. In 1324 a Korean printer published a work on the sayings of Confucius, with some movable type in its production.

Gutenberg took these earlier inventions and perfected a system of movable type for the European alphabet. It was flexible, cheap and practical, so it was rapidly adopted across Europe and led to a revolution in communication. *Rupert Matthews*

10 Literary works written in prison

Well, you've got to do something to pass the time, haven't you?

1 *Travels*
Marco Polo (1254–1324)

2 *Le Morte d'Arthur*
Thomas Malory (d. 1471)

3 *History of the World*
Walter Raleigh (c.1552–1618)

4 *The Pilgrim's Progress*
John Bunyan (1628–88)

5 *Hymn to the Pillory*
Daniel Defoe (c.1660– c.1731)

6 *Fanny Hill*
John Cleland (1709–89)

7 *Justine*
Marquis de Sade (1740–1814)

8 *De Profundis*
Oscar Wilde (1854–1900)

9 *Mein Kampf*
Adolf Hitler (1889–1945)

10 *Glimpses of World History*
Jawaharlal Nehru (1889–1964)

In Robert Browning's poem 'How They Brought the Good News from Ghent to Aix', what is the good news?

Ever since Browning's poem was first published, people have been speculating about the story behind it. The truth seems to be that the poet made it up. In a letter of 1883 Browning acknowledges that he had no specific incident in mind, but intended a merely general impression of warfare and sieges in medieval Flanders. *Nick Rennison*

Is there any truth in the story that Vincent Van Gogh once rented a studio in west London?

In his early twenties, Van Gogh, then planning a career as an evangelical preacher, lived and worked as a teacher in Isleworth, at that date (1876) a village. There is no record of his renting a studio there – he would have been unable to afford it and did not then consider himself an artist – but sketches of local scenes that he made at the time survive. *Nick Rennison*

Why did Robin Hood wear Lincoln green when he came from Nottinghamshire, or maybe Yorkshire, but definitely not Lincolnshire?

During the Middle Ages, Lincoln was a major centre for cloth manufacture. Several types of Lincoln cloth were produced – the most valuable was Lincoln scarlet – and they were used throughout England. It was entirely unsurprising that writers imagined Robin and his Merry Men dressed in Lincoln green – as unsurprising as a modern writer imagining characters today wearing blue jeans. The associations of green with nature and the forest made it an even more appropriate colour for the outlaw. *Nick Rennison*

Who was Mrs Grundy and why did she become the personification of prudery?

Mrs Grundy was not a real individual but a character in a now little-known play by a dramatist named Thomas Morton. She was mentioned by other characters in the play *Speed the Plough*, first produced in 1798, who worried constantly about what Mrs Grundy might think, but she didn't make an appearance on stage. During the 19th century her name became synonymous with a kind of middle-class propriety and unthinking prudishness. *Nick Rennison*

When did the Leaning Tower of Pisa begin to lean? And why was it built?

The Leaning Tower of Pisa was built as a campanile or freestanding bell-tower. It began to lean almost as soon as it was started in 1173 because of the nature of the ground on which its foundations were built. Construction of the tower was halted five years later, but was renewed at various times over the next two centuries. Each new attempt involved efforts to correct the 'lean' but all failed.
Nick Rennison

In Jane Austen's *Emma* there is a passing reference to Astley's, which was clearly some kind of theatre. What exactly was it?

Opened in the late 18th century by a former riding school owner and cavalry soldier named Philip Astley, Astley's Amphitheatre stood near Westminster Bridge and was a venue for elaborate feats of horsemanship and the restaging of famous battles. Part circus and part theatre-on-horseback, the shows at Astley's remained popular long after Philip Astley's death in 1814. The amphitheatre was only finally demolished in the 1890s. *Nick Rennison*

When did people stop writing with feathers, and why?

Steel nibs replaced quills as the writing instruments of choice in the 19th century. Quills were OK when comparatively few people wrote, but they could be expensive (the best came from live geese and swans) and they had to be cut correctly. And would you relish the task of plucking one of the five biggest feathers from the wing of a live goose? Thought not.

Metal nibs had been around for a long time (Samuel Pepys and Daniel Defoe both mention them), but they didn't really catch on until the mid-19th century, when a rapid expansion in literacy, record-keeping and public schooling inspired improvements in their quality and flexibility, and machine production techniques became more efficient.

Many early steel nib pens were produced in Birmingham, and among the most popular was the so-called 'dip pen', which consisted of a wood, glass or bone shaft with a (usually) interchangeable steel nib that you recharged by dipping into ink. Although long since eclipsed by fountain pens and ballpoints, the dip pen survived well into the 20th century. Many of the 'baby

boomer' generation will remember using them, while even younger readers will have sat at school desks that contained the holes to hold ceramic or plastic inkwells. Dip pens are still used by calligraphers, cartoonists and illustrators, usually because they can be filled with specialist inks that would damage a fountain pen. Actually, some specialist calligraphers will tell you that nothing writes as well as a hand-cut goose quill. *Eugene Byrne*

Is the Old Curiosity Shop in London the one Dickens knew?

Despite what is claimed on the awning above it, the shop in Portsmouth Street, near Lincoln's Inn Fields, has nothing to do with Dickens's novel. The shop would have been known to Dickens, since it dates back several centuries, but at the end of the novel, he says that his Old Curiosity Shop has been demolished. The shop in Portsmouth Street was only renamed the Old Curiosity Shop in 1868, nearly 30 years after Dickens's novel was first published. *Nick Rennison*

10 Writers banned by Vatican censors and put on the Index Librorum Prohibitorum

The Catholic church was no fan of the following wordsmiths:

1 **Thomas Hobbes**
(1588–1679) All works banned

2 **Samuel Richardson**
(1689–1761) *Pamela*

3 **François Voltaire**
(1694–1778) *Lettres Philosophiques, Histoires des Croisades, Cantiques des Cantiques*

4 **Jean-Jacques Rousseau**
(1712–78) *The Social Contract*

5 **Laurence Sterne**
(1713–68) *A Sentimental Journey*

6 **Edward Gibbon**
(1737–94) *History of the Decline and Fall of the Roman Empire*

7 **Honoré de Balzac**
(1799–1850) All completed works

8 **George Sand**
(1804–76) All love stories

9 **Gustave Flaubert**
(1821–80) *Madame Bovary, Salammbo*

10 **Jean-Paul Sartre**
(1905–80) All works

Which empire does the Empire State Building refer to?

The simple answer is that the building is named after the state in which it's located, New York State, which has long been nicknamed the 'Empire State'. The longer answer, of course, involves the reasons why the state is so called, and that's a bit trickier to explain.

There are two main contenders for the origins of the nickname. One is that Henry Hudson, who sailed up the river that now bears his name and into New York Bay in 1609, was so taken with the beauty and richness of the landscape that he declared, 'This is the new empire.' In this context it seems that Hudson refers not to a specific empire, but to the fact that the landscape itself seemed to hold all the natural riches and majesty of an empire.

The second possibility is that George Washington, the commander-in-chief of the continental forces in the 1775–83

American Revolution, and later the first president of the newly independent United States, was also so impressed with the state's natural abundance and diversity that when passing through it in 1784, he said that it was 'at present the seat of the empire'. Presumably, he meant the British Empire, though quite why he said this when the 13 Colonies had just fought a long and exhausting war to break free from said empire is less clear. Another possibility is that he has been misquoted and what he actually said was 'the seat of empire', meaning it in the same sense as Henry Hudson.
Steph Gapper

In the folk song 'Four Loom Weaver' there is the line: 'And Waterloo Porridge were best to us (as) food.' What is Waterloo Porridge and what are its associations with Waterloo?

The song is a traditional one, describing the dire poverty experienced by Lancashire cotton weavers in the early 19th century: 'I'm a four loom weaver, as many a man knows/I've nowt to eat and I've worn out my clothes/My clogs are all broken, and stockings I've none/Thee'd hardly gi's tuppence for all I've gotten on.' It was hugely popular in its time, with several versions (including an Irish one). Part of it is also quoted in Elizabeth Gaskell's 1848 novel *Mary Barton*. Joseph Wright's seminal *English Dialect Dictionary* tells us that Waterloo Porridge was oatmeal porridge made with water only – thin gruel, in other words. (It was also apparently a slang term for 'a good beating'.) The historian Martha Vicinus suggests that Waterloo Porridge could also refer to stale bread in hot water.

The weavers' plight resulted from industrialisation and the steam-powered machinery that made their skills redundant. Furthermore, the economic downturn in the years following the end of the Napoleonic Wars made conditions especially harsh for many working people; this was the era of Luddites, Reform riots and, later, the Chartists.

The Napoleonic Wars ended dramatically with the Battle of Waterloo in 1815, and it's possible that the name acknowledges the battle's part in the start of the bad times. It's just as likely that it is an ironic expression meant to be used with emphasis on the first two syllables. *Eugene Byrne*

When was the first London A–Z published? And who created it?

A young woman called Phyllis Pearsall compiled the first edition in the 1930s. She rose at 5 a.m. each day and walked 30 kilometres (18 miles) through the streets, taking notes, and eventually

completing 23,000 street entries, which she kept in shoe boxes under her bed. No publisher was interested, so she published it herself, delivering copies to branches of WH Smith in a wheelbarrow. By the time she died in 1996, the *A–Z* had sold millions of copies. *Nick Rennison*

Is it true that London once had its own Colosseum?

The Colosseum was a large rotunda in what is now Cambridge Terrace, near Regent's Park, designed by Decimus Burton and built in the 1820s. It contained a vast panorama of London, based on drawings made by Thomas Hornor from a wooden observatory erected above the ball and cross on top of St Paul's dome. Hornor and his backer ran up huge debts and promptly absconded to avoid their creditors. The Colosseum also tempted visitors with a Hall of Mirrors, a Gothic aviary and a Swiss chalet with a panorama of Mont Blanc. By the 1860s the building had fallen into disrepair and it was demolished in 1875. *Nick Rennison*

Can you tell me the significance of the unicorn denoting a 'perfect knight'?

The unicorn in its current Western form goes back to the Middle Ages, where it was a beautiful white creature with the body of a horse (as opposed to the goat-like creature or monster it was in some earlier myths). Its horn was thought to be capable of neutralising any poison, and the animal itself was a symbol of purity (sometimes also a symbol of virility), and was often associated with the Virgin Mary. In the age of chivalry it was a solitary, elusive animal that could be approached only by a virgin, so if you wanted to catch one, you'd use a maiden as bait. If a non-virgin tried to capture one, it would resist savagely and to the death.

The unicorn started appearing as a heraldic symbol in the 15th century for obvious reasons: it's a horse with a big sword and (in heraldry, at least) the tail of a lion. It's pure (and/or virile) and noble, and thus represents everything the knight would want to be. As John Guillim wrote in his 1610 work *A Display of Heraldry*, 'The greatness of his mind is such that he rather chooseth to die than be taken alive: wherein the unicorn and the valiant-minded soldier are alike.' *Eugene Byrne*

Henry VIII allegedly wrote 'Greensleeves' for Anne Boleyn. Have any other unlikely historical characters penned songs?

We're not certain that Henry did compose 'Greensleeves', but we know that he did write several other songs. Of course, writing and performing music were pastimes of the leisured classes across several historical periods and cultures. Henry was a Renaissance prince, aspiring to excel in all the arts, and is famous for 'Greensleeves' because it remains a much-loved ditty, while the compositions of others are long forgotten. Few now remember, say, Prime Minister George Canning's song in praise of William Pitt the Younger ('The Pilot that Weathered the Storm'). Likewise, only serious music aficionados know that J.S. Bach's *Musical Offering* was based on a theme by Frederick the Great of Prussia, a passionate amateur musician.

It's more usual nowadays for musicians to progress on to other careers: Bob Geldof, for example, campaigns against famine, and Sonny Bono was elected to Congress. Grateful Dead lyricist John Perry Barlow was one of the founders of the Electronic Frontier Foundation, campaigning to preserve free speech in the digital age. Oddest of all is former Steely Dan/Doobie Brothers guitarist Jeff 'Skunk' Baxter, who is also a consultant to the Pentagon on counter-terrorism and missile defence.

It looks like Henry remains the only significant figure in Western history to pen (allegedly) a genuine hit. But as bizarre crossover talents go, it still doesn't come even close to 1940s' Hollywood actress Hedy Lamarr patenting a frequency-switching system for guided torpedoes. *Eugene Byrne*

What was the Euston Arch?

This was the original entrance to Euston Station. Designed by Sir Philip Hardwick and first erected in 1837, it had Doric columns and was 22 metres (72 feet) high. It became a much-loved London landmark, and there was uproar when British Rail, claiming that it stood in the way of progress and new platforms, announced that it would be demolished. Despite a campaign to save it, led by the poet John Betjeman, Euston Arch was knocked down in 1962. *Nick Rennison*

10 Notable people who were also librarians

If you thought librarians were dull and dusty, then just think again.

1 **John Dee**
(1527–1608) scientist and astrologer

2 **Gottfried Leibniz**
(1646–1716) philosopher

3 **David Hume**
(1711–76) philosopher

4 **Giacomo Casanova**
(1725–98) womaniser

5 **August Strindberg**
(1849–1912) Swedish playwright

6 **Marcel Duchamp**
(1887–1968) artist

7 **Mao Zedong**
(1893–1976) statesman

8 **J. Edgar Hoover**
(1895–1972) FBI head

9 **Philip Larkin**
(1922–85) poet

10 **John Braine**
(1922–86) novelist

Did the Great Sphinx of Giza really lose its nose when Napoleon's soldiers in Egypt shot a cannon at it?

It's often claimed that bored French soldiers took pot-shots at the Sphinx, but earlier images of the monument indicate that it had lost its nose long before Napoleon arrived in Egypt. A 15th-century Muslim historian had a different tale to tell. He said a Sufi fanatic destroyed the nose because he was outraged that the peasants made offerings to the Sphinx. The truth is that the nose was probably just a victim of six millennia of erosion by wind and weather. *Nick Rennison*

When did we first start to call knockabout comedy 'slapstick', and why?

The word derives from the *battacchio*, a paddle-like object consisting of two wooden slats, which, when struck, produced a loud smacking noise. It was used in Italian *commedia dell'arte* performances from the 16th to the 18th century to suggest that actors were hitting one another violently when they were doing nothing of the sort. Translated into English as 'slapstick', it began to be used as a term for farcical physical comedy in the late 19th century. *Nick Rennison*

What is Britain's oldest existing newspaper?

The *London Gazette*, which is published Monday to Friday, covering statutory and government business, started in 1665 in Oxford, where Charles II and his court had fled to escape the plague. It's now published under the superintendence of Her Majesty's Stationery Office, and carries news of parliamentary and government activity, appointments, awards and honours. It also details military promotions and appointments, hence the term 'to be gazetted'.

Lloyd's List, which started at a London coffee house in 1734, is probably closer to most people's idea of what a newspaper looks like. Now, as then, it specialises in shipping and commerce news.

Among mass-market titles, the earliest are the *Daily Universal Register*, founded in 1785, which became *The Times* three years later, and the *Observer*, launched in 1791, which claims to be the world's first Sunday newspaper. These are pre-dated by several

10 Collapsing cathedrals

They sure knew how to build in those days...or did they?

1 **Winchester**
central tower collapsed,
1107

2 **Lincoln**
flattened by an earthquake,
1185

3 **St David's**
tower bit the dust,
1220

4 **Lincoln**
central tower fell down,
1237

5 **Ely**
curtains for main tower,
1322

6 **St Andrews**
south transept went west,
1409

7 **Lincoln**
rebuilt central spire
blew down, 1549

8 **Ripon**
central spire fell through
the roof, 1660

9 **Hereford**
west front disintegrated,
1786

10 **Chichester**
spire crashed to the ground,
1861

provincial papers, of which the earliest were *Berrow's Worcester Journal* and the *Stamford Mercury* (now the *Rutland & Stamford Mercury*). Both began in the 1690s, but weren't on a regular footing until the early 1700s. Other oldies include the *Newcastle Journal* (1711), the *Northampton Mercury* (1720), the *News Letter* (Belfast, 1737), *Press & Journal* (Aberdeen, 1747) and the *Yorkshire Post* (1754). The world's oldest continuously published newspaper is Sweden's *Post-och Inrikes Tidningar*, dating from 1645. As of 1 January this year it ceased to publish in print and became an Internet operation. *Eugene Byrne*

Why was Versailles constructed? What were the motives of Louis XIV in undertaking such a massive enterprise?

Versailles began as a hunting lodge for King Louis XIII, who reigned in France from 1610 to 1643. A similar love of princely outdoor pursuits drew his son Louis XIV (r. 1643–1715) to this heavily forested and marshy location. From 1666 this enthusiasm, and painful memories of his mother's lingering illness at the Louvre in the heart of Paris, led Louis XIV to spend more time at the country palace of Saint-Germain-en-Laye to the west of the city. Yet by the mid-1670s it was clear that it lacked sufficient space for the expanding royal court, and for Louis' landscaping and architectural ambitions.

From the early 1660s Versailles had been renovated to allow royal sojourns, but in 1677 the decision was taken to base the royal court in this location. A team of gardeners, architects and artists gradually descended on the small chateau and transformed it into the largest and most splendid palace in Europe, though the effort would take up the rest of Louis' reign. The court moved there for good in 1682, and in 1684 the king decided to expand the palace further still to accommodate more courtiers and ministerial bureaux under its roof. The scale of the undertaking at Versailles suited Louis XIV's political and personal interests: the palace itself was an awe-inspiring act of conspicuous consumption, and the fact that it remained a building site suited Louis' image as 'le roi architecte'. However, the emergence from near-wilderness of its model classical gardens, on which Louis himself wrote a visitors' guide, was the ultimate pharaonic conceit – the taming of nature by man. *Guy Rowlands*

I have heard that one of the first European archaeologists in Egypt was an ex-circus strongman. Is this true?

Giovanni Belzoni, born in Padua in 1778, landed in Egypt just after the Napoleonic Wars and collected many of the Egyptian artefacts now on display in the British Museum. A giant of a man, he left Italy following the French invasion of Rome in 1798 and went to England, where he worked as a circus strongman, often billed (misleadingly) as the Patagonian Samson. *Nick Rennison*

I recently saw a picture showing various historical places and persons connected with York. One of them was Richard III, who was shown with a white boar. What is the significance of the boar?

The white boar was the personal badge of the much-maligned Richard, younger brother of Edward IV, from the days when he was Duke of Gloucester. By the late 15th century heraldry had become a complex and highly refined science as well as an art. Heralds allowed families to impale (mix) their arms with those to which they married, and they delighted in inventing ways of distinguishing one brother from another by tiny variations. As a result, coats of arms tended to be both complex and confusing. Brothers and cousins could have remarkably similar coats of arms, while another brother might have impaled his arms with those of his wife to produce something very different. This was all very well for heralds who were thoroughly immersed in the study of heraldry, but it created all sorts of problems for everyday folk. To get around these issues of misidentification, many noblemen took personal badges in addition to their official coat of arms. These badges tended to be simple and distinctive. They were embroidered on to the clothes of servants and retainers, and painted on to property and buildings. They marked ownership without possibility of confusion. We do not know why Richard chose a wild boar, but he might have been attracted by the tenacious ferocity of the creature. Certainly the colour white was in reference to the white rose of York, from which dynasty Richard III came. *Rupert Matthews*

In the poem 'The Akond of Swat' Edward Lear asks, 'Who or which or why or what is the Akond of Swat?' Is there a real historical answer to his question?

Swat was a princely state in what is now Pakistan. Abdul Ghafur (c.1794–1877) was its religious leader, known as the Akhund. The Akhund had great influence over Muslims in the region at the time of the Indian Mutiny in 1857. His name would have appeared regularly in newspaper reports in the middle decades of the 19th century. Lear's verse was first published in 1877, although it was written earlier. He might have seen references to the Akond (sic) of Swat in the press and noted its potential for nonsense rhymes. *Nick Rennison*

I have read somewhere that a time capsule is buried under Cleopatra's Needle in London. Is this true?

Cleopatra's Needle was erected on the Embankment in 1878 after a proposed Westminster site was rejected. At the time, various items were placed in its plinth as a memorial of the day. These included newspapers, a copy of *Bradshaw's Railway Guide*, a portrait of Queen Victoria, pictures of 12 of the country's leading beauties, several bibles, a complete set of British coins from that year and a copy of the 1878 *Whitaker's Almanack*. *Nick Rennison*

CHAPTER 4

WORK AND LEISURE, OR THE DISORDERLY CARMAN

Who invented the yo-yo?

The yo-yo is one of the oldest toys in the world, and there is a Greek vase of the 5th century BC that shows a boy playing with a disc on a string, which looks remarkably like a modern yo-yo. The word itself comes from the Philippines, and it was a Filipino called Pedro Flores who introduced the toy to the USA in the 1920s and began the first yo-yo craze. *Nick Rennison*

From the 1901 census I found that my great-grandfather was a carman. What is it exactly?

The term 'carman' goes back to the Middle Ages (at least) and it simply means a 'carrier' – someone who drives a cart, often referred to as a 'carr' in earlier times. That's probably not too helpful in telling you any more about what your great-grandfather got up to during the working day. If he'd been a 'drayman', for example, he would probably have worked for a brewery; a dray was simply a low-sided cart designed for heavy loads, but by the early 20th century the term was usually applied only to vehicles delivering beer or mineral water. Had he been described as a 'carter', it's more likely that his job was rural rather than urban.

Just as nowadays there are tens of thousands of people who drive trucks and vans for a living, so there were similar numbers,

10 Famous beekeepers

Movers and shakers whose leisure time was a veritable hive of activity — the following people were all keen apiarists.

1 **Aristotle**
(384–322 BC) philosopher

2 **George Washington**
(1732–99) president

3 **Gregor Mendel**
(1822–84) geneticist

4 **Leo Tolstoy**
(1828–1910) author

5 **Robert Baden Powell**
(1857–1941) scout

6 **Raymond Poincaré**
(1860–1934) politician

7 **Henry Fonda**
(1905–82) actor

8 **Sir Edmund Hillary**
(1919–2008) mountaineer

9 **Sylvia Plath**
(1932–63) poet

10 **Sir Peter de la Billière**
(b. 1934) general

self-employed or (more usually) employees, in Edwardian times. Aside from those employed by shops and factories for deliveries, huge numbers worked for Britain's railway companies and docks. As well as moving goods, a carman was usually also responsible for looking after and grooming his horse(s). Since earliest times, carmen were blamed and reviled for causing traffic congestion, particularly in London, and for their assertive behaviour. In 1617, in an attempt to reduce the 'disorder and rude behaviour of Carmen, Draymen and others using Cartes', some one-way streets were established in London. Some people nowadays talk about white-van drivers in exactly the same terms! *Eugene Byrne*

Why do hatters have a reputation for being mad?

For centuries hatters used mercury compounds extensively in the process of turning fur and felt into hats. Mercury is a cumulative poison, and its effects include trembling, memory loss, depression, anxiety and mood swings – all things that would have contributed to the idea of mad hatters.
Nick Rennison

Who founded London Zoo?

The Zoological Society of London was founded in 1826 by
Sir Stamford Raffles, the empire-builder, and included many
famous scientists among its original members. Raffles died
the same year, but the Society, under the presidency of the
Marquis of Lansdowne, opened its collection to its Fellows in
1828, and to paying members of the public in 1847.
Nick Rennison

Everyone knows about blacksmiths, but I recently came across a reference to a whitesmith. What did he do?

The whitesmith was a fellow craftsman to the blacksmith, but
whereas the blacksmith worked in iron, the whitesmith
fashioned tin, pewter and other soft metals in his forge. In
Dickens's *Great Expectations* Joe Gargery muses
philosophically on a world in which 'one man's a blacksmith
and one man's a whitesmith and one man's a coppersmith and
one man's a goldsmith'. *Nick Rennison*

10 Royal hobbies

Find out how our monarchs have kept themselves amused over the centuries.

1 **Edward II**
(1284–1327) thatching

2 **Henry VI**
(1421–71) praying

3 **Elizabeth I**
(1533–1603) chess

4 **Mary Queen of Scots**
(1542–87) billiards

5 **Charles I**
(1600–49) bowls

6 **Charles II**
(1630–85) fishing

7 **William III and Mary II**
(1650–1702 and 1662–94) gardening

8 **George II**
(1683–1760) genealogy

9 **George III**
(1738–1820) astronomy

10 **Victoria**
(1819–1901) writing

10 People who had accidents on the job

Workplace mishaps sealed their fates.

1 **William of Sens**
   mason, fell from scaffold
   in Canterbury Cathedral,
   1179

2 **James II**
   king, killed when one of
   his own cannons blew up in
   his face,
   1460

3 **Jean-Baptiste Lully**
   composer, died from toe
   wound caused by beating
   time on the floor,
   1687

4 **Henry Winstanley**
   engineer, swept away
   with his Eddystone
   Lighthouse,
   1703

5 **George Basevi**
   architect, fell from roof of
   Ely Cathedral,
   1845

6 **William Bullock**
   antiquary, died after his leg
   got trapped in the printing
   press he had invented,
   1867

7 **John Roebling**
   engineer, died after his foot
   was crushed during the
   building of Brooklyn Bridge,
   1869

8 **Humphrey Jennings**
   film-maker, fell off cliff while
   scouting for locations in Greece,
   1950

9 **Mal 'King Kong' Kirk**
   wrestler, died after being
   landed on by 365-lb wrestler
   'Big Daddy',
   1987

10 **Brandon Lee**
   actor, shot while filming
   The Crow,
   1993

Why is it that doctors are called Dr but surgeons are called Mr (or the female equivalent)?

The title 'doctor' has a convoluted history, one of its original meanings being someone who had achieved the highest degree from a university. Because the early medical schools required students to complete a long, theoretical course in logic, philosophy and theology as well as medicine, they achieved this title. Surgery, however, was a rudimentary and messy practice, often carried out by barbers and quacks. Training was given by guilds, and surgeons did not require a university degree. Surgery was generally looked down upon by physicians and the clergy, who also practised medicine but were forbidden to 'make the cut' by the Fourth Lateran Council in 1215.

Medicine remained theoretical, based on the classical texts of Galen and Hippocrates, until the experimental revolution of the 17th and 18th centuries and the consequent advances in anatomy and physiology. But it was not until the introduction of anaesthesia and antiseptic procedures from 1846, which led to major surgical advances, that surgery began to be regarded as a respectable branch of medicine. These days the situation is reversed, and members of the Royal College of Surgeons omit the title of 'doctor' as a badge of pride since surgery has become one of the most specialised and demanding areas of medicine.
Steph Gapper

What was a villein in the Middle Ages, and is it connected to the modern word 'villain'?

In feudal England a villein was a peasant who was legally bound to a particular manor and, in effect, owned by the lord of that manor. The peasant was viewed as someone of less than knightly status and therefore not chivalrous. The word comes from the Latin *villanus*, meaning 'a worker on a country estate'.
Nick Rennison

I have a photo that shows 1930s' children playing on a beach with Tower Bridge in the background. Can you explain?

Tower Beach was deliberately created for the children of London's East End in 1934, when thousands of tons of sand were piled on the mud flats between St Katharine's Steps and the Tower. The chance for children to enjoy the seaside without leaving London lasted until 1971, when the beach closed.
Nick Rennison

If Romans wore sandals, how did they keep their feet warm in Britain?

Roman sandals were a little different from what we think of as sandals today. Although they generally had openwork toes, they tended also to have hefty soles, often with hobnails in, so they were chunkier than your average flip-flop. Remember that Roman legionaries used to march 30 kilometres (20 miles) a day in them, so they were sturdy enough for that. Nevertheless, a sandal designed for Mediterranean climes wasn't ideal British winter footwear. Evidence that the Romans who came here were only too aware of this fact has been found at Vindolanda fort. This Roman outpost to the south of Hadrian's Wall is famous for the wooden writing tablets found here during excavations. These tablets, dating to *c*. AD 100, show the everyday correspondence of the soldiers at the fort. One tablet includes the line, 'I send you socks and underpants' – proof that these Romans at least needed something warm inside their sandals. Vindolanda archaeologists have even managed to find one of the socks in question. Two fragments of wool, woven together and again dating to around AD 100, have been found there. Modern commentators consider socks and sandals a fashion faux-pas, but for a Roman legionary shivering through a Northumbrian winter, I think we can forgive the sartorial slip-up.
Dave Musgrove

When were the first garden gnomes made?

Garden gnomes might well have originated in Thuringia (Germany) in the early 1800s, but the first person to introduce them to Britain was an eccentric English baronet named Sir Charles Isham. He brought back 21 such terracotta figures from a trip to Germany in 1847 and placed them in the garden of Lamport Hall, his family house in Northamptonshire. One of the original gnomes, called 'Lampy', still survives and was recently insured for £1 million. *Nick Rennison*

10 Notable owners of poodles (and the names of their pets)

From intellectuals to soldiers, all have their fluffy side, it seems.

1 **Prince Rupert of the Rhine**
(1619–82) soldier and scientist:
Boy

2 **Arthur Schopenhauer**
(1788–1860) philosopher:
Atma

3 **Henry, Marquis of Worcester**
(1792–1853) soldier:
Sancho

4 **Gertrude Stein**
(1874–1946) writer and poet:
Basket

5 **Winston Churchill**
(1874–1965) statesman:
Rufus

6 **Thomas Mann**
(1875–1955) writer:
Niko

7 **Omar Bradley**
(1893–1981) D-Day general:
Beau

8 **John Steinbeck**
(1902–68) writer:
Charley

9 **Richard Nixon**
(1913–94) president:
Vicky

10 **Marilyn Monroe**
(1926–62) actress:
Maf(ia)

What did bear-baiting actually involve? Was it a game with rules, like cock-fighting?

Bear-baiting was popular in medieval England, but its heyday was the Tudor era. The animal would be chained to a post, and dogs – often mastiffs – were set to fight it. While the chain would give the bear some freedom of movement, it might be handicapped in other ways, such as having its claws removed. Older animals bore the scars and injuries of previous bouts, and some were blind. Large amounts of money were wagered on the outcome of fights. Although 'matches' took place all over the country, the most famous venue was the Bear Garden at Bankside in London, where in

1590 five bears were kept, along with several dogs, monkeys and bulls. At least three of the bears – Great Ned, Harry Hunks and Sackerson – were household names.

Both Henry VIII and Elizabeth I enjoyed bear-baiting, and when Elizabeth went on her progresses, towns would put on shows for her. At Kenilworth in 1575 the Earl of Leicester put on a spectacular involving 13 bears. When, in the 1590s, London's playhouses were drawing audiences away from bear-baiting, the council ordered theatres closed for two afternoons a week to keep bear-baiting in business. The Puritans, however, hated the 'sport', and it was banned under Cromwell. After the Restoration it never really enjoyed its previous popularity, and was finally abolished, along with bull-baiting, in 1835.
Eugene Byrne

10 Mining disasters

Between 1870 and 1930 about 1000 people a year were killed in Britain's mines.

1 **New Hartley, Newcastle**
204 killed,
16 January 1862

2 **Barnsley, Yorkshire**
361 killed,
12 December 1866

3 **Ferndale, Rhondda**
178 killed,
8 November 1867

4 **Blantyre, Lanarkshire**
207 killed,
22 October 1877

5 **Abercarn, Monmouthshire**
260 killed,
11 September 1878

6 **Llanerch, Monmouthshire**
176 killed,
6 February 1890

7 **Cilfnydd, Glamorgan**
290 killed,
23 June 1894

8 **Hulton, Lancashire**
344 killed,
21 December 1910

9 **Senghenydd, Glamorgan**
439 killed,
14 October 1913

10 **Gresford, Wrexham**
266 killed,
22 September 1934

Why are so many cinemas called 'Odeon'?

The famous Odeon cinema chain began in 1928 when the entrepreneur Oscar Deutsch opened his first picture house in the Midlands. According to his company's later publicity, the name Odeon stood for Oscar Deutsch Entertains Our Nation, but Deutsch had in fact taken the name from an ancient Greek word for a type of theatre. Other theatres and cinemas had been called Odeons before (the former Odéon Theatre in Paris was built in 1782), but it was Deutsch who made 'Odeon' almost synonymous with 'cinema'. *Nick Rennison*

CHAPTER 5

SPORT, OR THE CELEBRATED PEDESTRIAN

Who has won the most Olympic medals?

The athlete who has won the most Olympic medals is Larissa Latynina of the USSR. During the course of her gymnastics career, Latynina won a total of 18 medals: nine gold, five silver and four bronze. Born in 1934 in the Ukraine, she survived the German invasion of 1941, and after the war moved to attend school in Kiev. Latynina preferred ballet, but took up gymnastics after her ballet teacher moved. In 1953 she went to the Burevestnik Sports School, and the following year took part in the World Championships in Rome. There she was part of the USSR team that took the gold medal. At the Olympics of 1956 she won four golds. Four years later, at the Games in Rome, she led the Soviet Union team, taking three more golds. At her third Olympic Games, Latynina won two more gold medals, as well as adding to her collection of silvers and bronzes. Her Olympic record was unprecedented and has never been equalled. She won a medal in every event in which she competed, except for the 1956 balance beam, where she was placed fourth. Latynina took part in the 1966 World Championships, but then retired from active participation to become a coach for the Soviet gymnastics team. When the

Olympic Games took place in Moscow in 1980 she was put in charge of organising the gymnastics events, and is generally agreed to have done a fine job. In 2000 she was presented with the Order of Honour by Russian president Vladimir Putin. Latynina now lives just outside Moscow.

The country with the most Olympic medals is the USA, with a total of 2299, of which 931 were gold. This total has been helped by the fact that the USA has competed in all the modern games, while the country with the second highest tally, the USSR, competed only between 1952 and 1992.
Rupert Matthews

What is the history and background for horse races and local matches being called a 'derby'?

The Derby at Epsom, which is run on the first Saturday in June, is one of the classic British horse races. The race owes its name to Stanley Edward Smith, the 12th Earl of Derby (1752–1834). He was a passionate sportsman and heavy gambler, who enthused about a diverse range of sporting activities, including cricket, hunting, cockfighting and horse racing. In 1779 he initiated a new race at Epsom, which he called The Oaks after a stately home that was connected to him. Then, the following year, he began The Derby, which he gave his own name, ensuring his legacy for centuries to come. Over the years, several races around the globe adopted the name, probably the most well known being the Kentucky Derby in the United States. The use of the term 'derby' for a sporting contest played between local rivals is today fairly ubiquitous. It seems to have first appeared in the late 19th or early 20th century, but its origins remain uncertain. One popular theory is that the name relates to an old-fashioned football game that was traditionally played on Shrove Tuesday between the parishes of All Saints and St Peter's in Derbyshire. Some others believe that the source is actually the Derby horse race, but it is not entirely clear what the connection is, except perhaps to signify a sporting event of real significance. *Rob Attar*

While researching my family tree, I came across a local newspaper death notice from 1851 describing a (possible) ancestor as 'a celebrated pedestrian'. What does this mean?

Until the invention of the internal combustion engine, the term 'pedestrian' was usually applied to people who walked for sport. Competitive walking was quite common in the 18th and 19th centuries, with pedestrians from all walks of life performing prodigious feats for wagers or the proceeds of a collection from spectators. Champion walkers, such as Foster Powell, George Wilson and James Wathen, were minor celebrities in Georgian Britain, while Robert Barclay Allardice (1779–1854), known simply as Captain Barclay, was a household name. Barclay was a powerfully built athlete who trained with pedestrians and prize-fighters. His greatest feat, at Newmarket in 1809, was walking 1.6 kilometres (1 mile) each hour for 1000 consecutive hours. He lost over 13 kilograms (2 stone) in the process, but five days later he rejoined his regiment for the Walcheren expedition in perfect health. It was in his blood; his father was also a pedestrian, who once walked from Kincardineshire to London – 815 kilometres (510 miles) – in ten days.

The most interesting pedestrian is probably Mary McMullen, a mysterious working-class Irishwoman, who performed long-distance walks for crowds in England in the 1820s. She could walk 32 kilometres (20 miles) in four hours, and once did two 145-kilometre (92-mile) walks in four days. She was in her sixties at the time. *Eugene Byrne*

What was the first sporting event ever filmed?

In 1895, the same year that the Lumière brothers had their first film showing in Paris, the pioneering British movie-maker Birt Acres set up his camera at some major sporting events. He filmed The Derby in May of that year, and the University Boat Race two months earlier. So, in all likelihood, the Oxford v Cambridge Boat Race in 1895 was the first sporting event to be recorded for posterity on film. *Nick Rennison*

Is Chelsea's football ground (Stamford Bridge) named after the battle between King Harold and Harald Hardrada? And if so, why?

The great Battle of Stamford Bridge, on 25 September 1066, was fought on and around a bridge over the River Derwent at Stamford Bridge in Yorkshire. It was long and fierce, but ended with complete victory for King Harold of England. King Harald Hardrada of Norway, along with most of his army, was killed. The casualties suffered by the English, however, probably weakened their army and contributed to the victory of Duke William of Normandy at the rather more famous Battle of Hastings, fought just three weeks later.

Stamford Bridge football ground in west London would not at first glance seem to be linked to the medieval battle – after all, the clash of the Norwegian and English kings took place in Yorkshire. The ground was opened in 1877, as the home of the London Athletics Club, on the banks of the Stanford Creek, a tributary of the Thames, just north of a bridge that carried the Fulham Road over the narrow waterway. That bridge was known locally as the Sanford Bridge, but from the outset the stadium was called Stamford Bridge. It has been speculated, but not proven, that the Athletics Club named its stadium after the battle because it was keen to draw spectators from central London. History lessons of the period placed great emphasis on battles and kings, so the Battle of Stamford Bridge would have been widely known to Londoners. A familiar name might have helped to draw the crowds.
Rupert Matthews

Is it true that an English sportsman was once asked to become the King of Albania?

This might sound like something from the plot of an old adventure novel, but it is true according to the man himself. After the First World War the cricketer and all-round sportsman C.B. Fry was working as a diplomat at the League of Nations when the Albanians, short of a monarch, asked him if he would like the job. He declined. *Nick Rennison*

Why was Charles II nicknamed Old Rowley?

Charles II was a great enthusiast for horse-racing, and one of his favourite horses was a stallion called Old Rowley. The name was transferred to the king, probably because of Charles's legendary prowess as a lover. One of the racecourses at Newmarket is still called the Rowley Mile.
Nick Rennison

Is it right that the idea for the modern Olympic Games came from Shropshire?

Baron Pierre de Coubertin, founder of the modern Olympic Games, took his inspiration from the ancient Greeks, but he was also influenced by a visit in 1890 to Much Wenlock in Shropshire to see the 'Olympian' games regularly staged there by a local doctor, William Penny Brookes. *Nick Rennison*

10 Sports of Olympics past

Some of the Games' more unusual activities...

1 **Rope climbing**
   (four times
   between 1896
   and 1932)

2 **100m freestyle for sailors**
   (Athens 1896)

3 **Live pigeon shooting**
   (Paris 1900)

4 **Underwater swimming**
   (Paris 1900)

5 **High jump for horses**
   (Paris 1900)

6 **Standing high jump**
   (Paris 1900 and
   Stockholm 1912)

7 **56-pound weight throw**
   (St Louis 1904 and
   Antwerp 1920)

8 **Club swinging**
   (St Louis 1904 and L.A. 1932)

9 **Motorboat racing**
   (London 1908)

10 **Duelling pistol shooting**
   (Stockholm 1912)

I have heard that the first Australian cricket team to tour England was an Aboriginal one. Surely this can't be true?

Indeed it is true: a team of Aboriginal cricketers arrived in England in May 1868, ten years before the first white Australian national team. They won 14 out of 47 matches and were expected, after the cricket, to appear in 'native apparel' and demonstrate spear-throwing and boomerang-hurling.
Nick Rennison

Is it true that tug-of-war was once an Olympic sport?

Tug-of-war was part of the Olympic programme from 1900 to 1920. Britain twice won gold medals in the event – in 1908 and 1920. In the 1908 games, held in London, a team from the City of London police was victorious, although there was controversy earlier in the competition when the Americans withdrew because they claimed another British team, from Liverpool, was cheating.
Nick Rennison

Are there any other nations that have a sporting rivalry similar to that between England and Germany?

Many pairs of nations have rivalries, both friendly and ill-tempered, that extend back many years. Two of the most prominent are in Latin America. In 1969 the football rivalry between El Salvador and Honduras took an ugly and fatal turn. In June the two states were drawn against each other for a World Cup qualifying play-off. During the match, played in El Salvador, Honduran fans were beaten up, the Honduran flag burnt, and abusive slogans chanted by the home crowd. In Honduras the population responded by launching a series of riots in which the Salvadoran vice-consul was attacked, thousands injured and dozens killed. Vast crowds of Salvadorans began fleeing Honduras. At dawn on 14 July the Salvadoran air force began bombing targets in Honduras, while the navy landed forces on offshore islands and the army launched a major land invasion. The Organisation of American States moved quickly to impose an armistice, but not before around 2000 people, mostly Honduran civilians, had been killed. The border between the two states remained closed for some time, and free movement was not restored for almost a decade. El Salvador won the replay of the interrupted match (held in Mexico) 3–2.

By comparison, the rivalry between Brazil and Paraguay seems almost tame, though it is of much longer standing. Its most recent upsurge came in 2001, during another World Cup qualifying fixture. During the weeks leading up to the match, the Brazilian media ran some fiery stories, dragging up past sporting grievances and dubbing the forthcoming fixture 'war on the pitch'. The Paraguayan captain hit back on the eve of the match, telling a television interviewer, 'If we're going to talk about war, let's hope that Brazil returns the lands it took from Paraguay.' He was referring to some territory seized after a war that ended in 1870, and that has remained a major issue between the two countries. The remarks inflamed the situation even further, and it took weeks before the press let the subject drop. Brazil eventually won the match 2–0. *Rupert Matthews*

What is the highest number of world records broken at a single athletics meeting?

In recent years sporting world records have tended to be broken most often at large, prestigious sporting events. This is because the athletes concerned have training regimes that are designed to peak their performances at the major sporting events, where press coverage is guaranteed to be enormous. The rewards of sponsorship that flow from success at these venues make the effort worthwhile. It comes as no surprise, therefore, that the 2008 Beijing Olympics saw the unprecedented number of 43 world records broken. The record-breaking star of the games was Michael Phelps of the USA, who broke seven world records in the swimming pool. Indeed, it was in the swimming events that most records were broken. In all, 25 new swimming world records were set, along with 66 new Olympic records (some of them being the record for the same event broken several times in successive races). There was one Olympic race in which the first five finishers broke the old world record. The cause of the mass tumbling of swimming records was not so much an improvement among athletes as an improvement of technology. The LZR Racer swimsuit made by Speedo reduced drag by an astonishing

24 per cent both by hugging the swimmer's body and setting up a very thin layer of turbulent water over the suit's surface.

Before the days of technology-driven improvements and suspicions of substance abuse, the most spectacular sporting event so far as world records is concerned was the meeting held at Ann Arbor, Michigan, on 25 May 1935. At 3.25 p.m. athlete Jesse Owens broke the World long jump record. At 3.45 p.m. he broke the World 200 metres (220 yards) sprint record. At 4 p.m. he broke the 200 metre low hurdles record. In these last two races he completed the first 200 metres in times that broke those world records as well, making a total of five world records for one man in just 35 minutes! *Rupert Matthews*

An American friend from Philadelphia emailed me recently claiming that his city had once produced one of the world's greatest cricketers. Surely Americans don't play cricket, and never have done?

In colonial times cricket, often known as 'wickets', was almost as popular in America as it was in England. Troops of the Continental Army, at the lowest point in its fortunes at Valley Forge, are supposed to have amused themselves playing it, and George Washington himself occasionally played. Cricket remained popular after Independence in the northeastern states, especially Pennsylvania. The USA and Canada played the first-ever international match, in September 1844 at St George's Cricket Club, New York; the game attracted 10,000–20,000 spectators over three days. Canada won.

The decline in American cricket is probably due to the increasing appeal of baseball. It's often claimed that baseball caught on during the Civil War because soldiers could hold an impromptu game anywhere, while cricket requires a carefully prepared ground. By the late 19th century cricket was also increasingly associated with wealthy patricians in the northeast, and came to be seen as snooty. Even the game's own upper-crust enthusiasts started abandoning it in favour of tennis and golf.

Your friend is probably referring to the much-loved John Barton ('Bart') King (1873–1965). Unusually for an American cricketer, King came from a relatively humble background.

While the sport declined elsewhere in the USA, it remained popular in Philadelphia, and it was as a member of the Philadelphian team that he spent most of his career, even touring England three times before the First World War. Many people – even in England – rated King as the best bowler of the age. One story about him claims that he was so irritated by the bragging of a batsman from a rival team that he ordered his own team back to the pavilion, saying he wouldn't need any fielders because he would bowl the blowhard out with the first ball – and he did. *Eugene Byrne*

What was the longest running race ever held?

The longest race ever held between human runners, and in all likelihood the longest that ever will be held, began on 31 March 1929 in New York City. The finishing tape was located 5850 kilometres (3635 miles) away in Los Angeles, California. On 17 June the winner, Johnny Salo of Finland, crossed the line, having been running for a total of 525 hours and 57 minutes. The rules allowed the runners to be on the road for up to eight hours per day. Salo had averaged 11.12 km/h (6.91 mph) over this distance. Astonishingly, the second placed runner, Britain's Peter Gavuzzi, came over the finishing line only 2 minutes and 47 seconds behind Salo. It was Salo's victory, and his subsequent successes in other long-distance races, that established Finland's reputation in the 1930s as a nation of runners and sportsmen.

The longest running race that is held on a regular basis is the 4989-kilometre (3100-mile) Sri Chinmoy Race, held annually in New York. The course consists of a looped layout, allowing the runners to run continually without disrupting traffic. The record for completing this race is 41 days 8 hours 16 minutes 29 seconds, achieved by Wolfgang Schwerk of Germany in 2006. Only one woman has ever completed the race, Suprabha Beckjord of the USA. By comparison, the 41 kilometres (26 miles) of the marathon seem tame indeed.
Rupert Matthews

What is the oldest sport still being played in Britain?

Obviously, people have always held running, jumping, throwing and fighting contests, while football and rugby can point to antecedents involving medieval mobs and pigs' bladders. But the oldest sport in terms of formal rules that remain recognisable today is arguably wrestling. Wrestling is very ancient, cropping up in many different cultures worldwide, including Japan, which has sumo, India, where it is mentioned in the *Mahabharata* and the *Epic of Gilgamesh*, and the Middle East, as evidenced in the Old Testament. In Britain it goes back at least to Celtic times; in some parts of England it was traditional for bouts to be held when the harvest had been taken in, or on Lammas Day (1 August). By the 19th century professional wrestlers were a regular feature of fairs, challenging all-comers to try to beat them. Later, wrestlers also featured on the bills at music halls, which partly explains why the sport turned into a 'variety act' that all but the most credulous spectator assumed was barely a competitive sport at all. It was hugely popular (and often very sleazy) in the 1920s and 1930s, and of course later gave us the televised golden age from the 1950s to the 1970s, with stars such as Big Daddy, Jackie Pallo and Giant Haystacks.

Despite the camp nature of the professional sport, and the arrival of even more stagey American-style wrestling at major venues and on our TV screens, you can still see amateurs wrestling to very old rules in some parts of the country. The two main centres of traditional wrestling in England are the southwest and the north. 'Cumbrian' wrestling, which has Viking origins, can be seen at country fairs, such as the Grasmere Sports & Show or the Cumberland Show. Meanwhile, traditional Celtic Cornish Wrestling still has plenty of enthusiasts and can be seen at summer events across the county, including the Royal Cornwall Agricultural Show. *Eugene Byrne*

Which sport was the first to be floodlit?

Floodlighting consists of a series of extremely high-powered lights that are used at night to 'flood' a large area of ground with illumination bright enough for spectators to watch a sports match taking place. The main motivation for floodlighting a sports arena has traditionally been so that spectators can attend winter matches in the evenings when they are free of work and other commitments. More recently, floodlighting has expanded rapidly as the demands of television schedules, and the huge income from advertising that they can command, have come to dominate.

The claim for the first sports match to be floodlit is traditionally disputed between Association Football and Rugby League. Both sports can claim a match to be lit by floodlighting in October 1878, but there is much dispute over which, if either, can be properly described as a 'floodlit match'. The first of the two was a demonstration soccer match held on 14 October at the Bramall Lane Ground, Sheffield, between two teams, the Reds and the Blues. Neither of these teams was a real sports team, as they were made up of players available on the day for the purposes of testing the floodlights. The match began before dark and the later stages were illuminated by four arc lamps supplied by Siemens.

The Rugby League claim rests on a regular match between two proper teams, Broughton and Swinton, which was held at the Broughton ground in Lancashire on 22 October. This was undoubtedly the first genuine sports fixture to be illuminated by floodlighting. However, at this date there was no such thing as mains electricity. All floodlights had to be powered by batteries or dynamos installed for the event. These were notoriously unreliable and often ineffective. By 1888 all these early experiments had been abandoned as unviable. Floodlighting did not return to major sports fixtures until Arsenal Football Club installed more modern versions in the late 1930s. The Second World War then intervened, with its blackout regulations. Floodlighting finally became a regular feature of sports matches in the 1950s. *Rupert Matthews*

Why is zero called 'love' in tennis, a 'duck' in cricket and 'nil' in football? What's wrong with nought, nothing or zero in all games?

It's often impossible to pin down the origins of sporting traditions and jargon, although if you want a neat thematic link between love and a duck, it's eggs. When the batsman is out for nothing in cricket he's said to have scored a duck because, according to cricketing tradition, of the resemblance of the zero on the scoreboard to a duck's egg. In tennis it's often claimed that 'love' comes from the French for 'egg' – *l'oeuf* – for similar reasons. But this assumes there ever was such a thing as a French tennis scoreboard in the 18th and 19th centuries, which there probably wasn't.

Another theory is that early French games used a clock face for scoring – 0, 15, 30, 40 – and that zero was the hour (*l'heure*) which became corrupted to 'love' in English. (So why did they score 40 and not 45 if using a clock face? The ever-more-tortured theory has it that the French preferred the sound of the 'quinze, trente, quarante' sequence.) The most convincing explanation of the origins of 'love' is that it's an old English usage, meaning 'nothing', as in 'play for love' (as opposed to a wager). Although modern lawn tennis was mostly devised and popularised by Major Walter Wingfield (1833–1912), it was based on much older French and English games, including rackets and real tennis, so maybe love goes back that far.

As for nil in football, it's a contraction of the Latin *nihil*, meaning 'nothing'. Nil was in widespread use in legal and financial circles and in everyday speak long before it became a footballing term. Interestingly enough, it's a very 'British' word that is little used by other English-speaking cultures. As for why they don't all use the same word for nothing, perhaps you'd better take that up with the governing bodies of the sports in question. *Eugene Byrne*

When was the first Football Pools competition?

In the spring of 1922 a former Coldstream Guards officer was trying to think of a way to earn a living having returned to civilian life following the First World War. After trying out a number of ideas, John Jervis Barnard came up with a novel method of allowing people to gamble on the outcome of football matches. Instead of betting a sum of money on whether or not a particular team would win in a single match, Barnard thought that it would be more interesting if people could bet on a range of options. His first plan was to print a list of all football matches due to take place on a particular Saturday. He then asked his customers to pick six teams that they thought would win their matches. A sliding scale of prizes was devised, with the highest prize going to a person who predicted six winners, less money to a person who predicted five winners and so forth. From his offices at 28 Martineau Street, Birmingham, Barnard placed a series of newspaper advertisements. At first only a few people took up the challenge, and for several weeks Barnard made a loss. When the new football season opened in the autumn of 1922, Barnard decided to give his idea one more try. He again placed his adverts and this time the orders came flooding in by the hundred, then by the thousand.

Barnard continued to run his business until he retired in 1938, when he sold out to a rival company called Cope's Pools. More successful than either Cope's Pools or Barnard was Littlewood Pools, founded in 1923 by a London telegraph operator named John Moores. The game devised by Moores was more complex, with different points being scored for a home win, away win, score draw or no score draw. This version of the game proved to be enormously popular, and within seven years Moores had earned £1 million. *Rupert Matthews*

I read recently that various kings in the Middle Ages regularly tried to ban people playing bowls. What was so morally corrupting about this pastime?

Monarchs periodically cracked down on pastimes that distracted the men from practising archery, though sometimes sports were restricted for fear of rowdiness and, in the case of bowls, because of gambling. The Scots, who laid down the modern rules of bowls in Victorian times, are said to have gambled on their games very rarely, so it was always much more respectable north of the border. We must be careful about interpreting restrictions because although

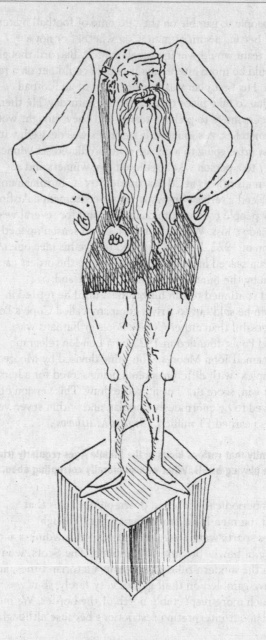

we know that bowls is an old sport in England (the Southampton Old Bowling Green dates back to 1299), medieval statutes in Latin could just as easily be referring to other ball games, or even stone-throwing contests similar to shot-putting.

The first use of the word 'bowls' doesn't occur until a law of 1511. Later, in 1541, the Act for the 'maintenance of artillery and the debarring of unlawful games' set out restrictions on bowls and other games, including 'logetting in the fields' and 'slide-thrift' (otherwise called 'shove-groat'). This law was indeed intended to keep men practising archery and to support the archery business. The Act specifically said that if highly skilled 'bowyers, fletchers, stringers and arrowhead makers' were not kept in employment in England, they might go to Scotland – England's enemy – in search of work. Once the bow and arrow were truly displaced by firearms, there's little evidence that the law was much enforced, though it remained on the statute books until the 1840s. Bowls remained popular with upper and lower classes alike, and part of its appeal was that it could be played by women. An Elizabethan courtier said that bowls was like life at court, with everyone competing to get closest to the queen, in the form of the jack – 'the nearest are the most spited, and all bowls aim at the one the other, to turn out of place'.
Eugene Byrne

Who was the oldest person ever to win a gold medal at the modern Olympics?

Swedish shooter Oscar Swahn has the greatest claim to being the oldest Olympian. Aged 60, he won a gold in 1912 in the strangely named 'running deer, single-shot' event. Four years later he returned to take another gold in a team event. In the first Olympics after the First World War, held in Antwerp in 1920, the indomitable Swahn, 72, was still competing, and won a silver medal. The long white beard he sports in photos of the medal ceremonies was clearly no impediment to him.
Nick Rennison

A friend down the pub says that the 1981 film *Escape to Victory*, featuring Michael Caine, Sylvester Stallone and Pelé as Allied PoWs playing a football match with their German captors, is based on a true story. Surely not?

The film is indeed based on true events, although it's actually so far from reality that it might as well be complete fiction. *Escape to Victory* (just *Victory* in the USA), directed by John Huston, starred Michael Caine, Sylvester Stallone, Max von Sydow, Pelé, Osvaldo Ardiles and Bobby Moore, plus Ipswich Town players as other footballers. Our heroes, Allied PoWs in the Second World War, are to play a German all-star team in Paris and are coached by former West Ham player John Colby (Caine). Some of them plan to use the game to escape...

The US film was based on a 1961 Hungarian movie called *Two Half Times in Hell*, inspired by events in Kiev in 1942. With the Germans in control of the Ukraine, some players from the hugely popular Dynamo Kiev football club teamed up with a few players from former local rivals Lokomotiv Kiev to form a new team called FC Start. Start thrashed teams put up by occupying German, Hungarian and Romanian garrisons. The Germans became concerned that Start's victories might affect the morale of the local populace, so decided to teach them a lesson. On 9 August 1942, Start played a Luftwaffe team at Dynamo's Zenit Stadium. Despite very dirty German play and a referee who was an SS officer, Start won 5–3. Near the end of the game, a Start defender took possession, got the ball all the way to the German goal-mouth, then showed his contempt for them by kicking it back to the centre. Shortly afterwards, several Start players were arrested, and at least one died under torture. The rest were sent to labour camps, where a number died. After the war, two Soviet films were also made about the story. Zenit Stadium was renamed Start Stadium in 1981, and a sculpture there commemorates the 'Death Match'.
Eugene Byrne

CHAPTER 6

FOOD AND DRINK, OR THE ORIGINS OF THE ENGLISH BREAKFAST

It's a cliché of movies and books that ship's biscuit in the days of sail was invariably infested with maggots and weevils. Is this a myth, or did our seafaring ancestors develop a taste for grubs in their grub?

It's partly true. Ship's biscuit, often also known as 'hard tack' (and by innumerable slang terms usually based on its hardness), is cheap, compact, easily stored and easy to produce. It's baked from flour, water and salt. It gradually went out of vogue in HM forces, partly because the invention of self-raising flour meant fresh bread could be baked at sea or during land campaigns without using yeast, which does not keep for long. At sea, biscuit was usually eaten after being dipped into water or beer, or was broken into pieces and put in stews, including the famous 'lobscouse' (a stew made from meat, vegetables and biscuit). Stored properly, biscuit can keep for years in all conditions. Even now, the Ministry of Defence is said to hold small quantities for long missions in remote areas. Museums have examples that are hundreds of years old. The National Maritime Museum has one with the date 1784 etched on it. Biscuit could get damp and spoilt, or be invaded by grubs, but this probably happened more on merchant ships with profiteering owners, where faster crew turnover and less disciplined procedures made infestation more of a hazard. *Eugene Byrne*

What are the origins of the English breakfast?

The 'full English', with bacon, eggs, sausages, tomatoes and its various side orders, is a fairly recent innovation. It should also more properly be known as the 'full British Isles breakfast' since the Scots, Welsh and Irish (both north and south) have similar ideas of a full breakfast, though with regional variations and additions. For example, breakfast is likely to include black pudding in the north of England, while in Scotland there may be square sausage, haggis and potato scones. In Ireland there's white pudding and soda bread, and Ulster includes its famous potato farls. A London caff might have bubble and squeak, while in Wales you might be offered laver bread. Menus like these were almost unknown before the 20th century, although wealthier folk sometimes breakfasted on bacon (or ham) and eggs since at least Tudor times. By the Victorian era the rich could eat prodigious breakfasts, with kippers, kedgeree, devilled kidneys and more. But the working classes ate whatever they could afford, which might be just porridge or bread.

The fried breakfast of bacon, eggs and perhaps sausages almost certainly originated with the late 19th- and early 20th-century middle classes. It was only with the prosperity (and end of food rationing) that came about in the 1950s and 1960s that fried breakfasts were available to all, and quickly became a favourite among manual workers, who frequented 'greasy spoon' cafés. In our more health-conscious times, few of us consume such meals every day. The full English is a treat for weekends and holidays. How the 'fried breakfast' or 'fry-up' became known as a 'full English' is a bit of a mystery. Our theory is that the term originated in the 1960s or 1970s, quite possibly in Mediterranean (or maybe even British) holiday resorts, where it would be advertised as such to vacationing Brits who found the 'continental breakfast' an unappetising disappointment. *Eugene Byrne*

Did Marie Antoinette ever really say, 'Let them eat cake'?

The story that Queen Marie Antoinette (1755–93), when told that people were dying from want of bread, replied, 'Let them eat cake,' is a familiar one, but there is no evidence that it is actually true. Jean-Jacques Rousseau, in his *Confessions*, refers to a similar story, but he ascribes the remark only to 'a great princess'. Since Marie Antoinette was only 12 years old when Rousseau wrote

Confessions, it is extremely unlikely that it was she of whom he was thinking. The probability is that a previously existing story was attached to Marie Antoinette's name during the French Revolution as part of the vicious propaganda campaign that revolutionaries directed at the French queen. *Nick Rennison*

Who invented Horlicks?

Unsurprisingly, it was a man named Horlick. William Horlick emigrated from his native England to the United States in the 1860s and later set up a company to make and market a malted milk drink. Horlicks was originally intended as a drink for babies, but it became much more popular with adults, who found its soporific effect made it an ideal nightcap. In fact, the explorer Richard Byrd, whose men had enjoyed the drink while they were on an Antarctic expedition, gratefully named a mountain range after Mr Horlick. *Nick Rennison*

Why were smugglers of illegal alcohol in Prohibition-era America called 'bootleggers'?

In the days when horsemen routinely wore long boots that covered the legs from the foot to above the knee, the 'bootleg' was a convenient place to hide everything from weapons to liquor. In the 1880s, traders in the American west who chose to smuggle bottles of illicit whisky to their Native American customers became known as 'bootleggers' because they used their boots as hiding places. The word was given much wider currency 40 years later, when it was applied to the gangsters of the Prohibition era. *Nick Rennison*

We all use the phrase 'the greatest thing since sliced bread', but when was sliced bread actually invented?

Otto Frederick Rohwedder was an American jewellery store owner who became obsessed with the idea that he could make his fortune by inventing an automatic bread-slicing machine. He worked on various prototypes from 1912 onwards, but it was not until 1928 that a baker in the small town of Chillicothe, Missouri, installed one of Rohwedder's machines in his bakery and began selling pre-sliced bread to the public. People loved it, and sliced bread became the greatest thing since... *Nick Rennison*

When did tea drinking become popular in England?

The first European to write about tea was a 16th-century Jesuit missionary from Portugal called Jasper de Cruz. He came across the drink during a visit to China. The Dutch took tea back to Europe later in the century, and it was in The Hague that the exiled Charles II first tasted it. Tea had been drunk occasionally in England during Cromwell's rule, yet it was after Charles's restoration in 1660 that it began to become widely popular. *Nick Rennison*

Why were American soldiers in the First World War called 'doughboys'?

The word dates back much further than the First World War. It was first recorded in the 1840s, but gained greater currency in the American Civil War when men of the Union infantry were often known as 'doughboys'. As early as the 17th century a 'doughboy' was a kind of small, flat, flour dumpling, and it has been suggested that the large brass buttons on the soldiers' uniforms reminded people of these dumplings. *Nick Rennison*

10 Favourites of the Tudor diet

The food and drink consumed in a year at the court of Henry VIII.

1	Wild boar	53
2	Barrels of wine	300
3	Calves	760
4	Oxen	1240
5	Pigs	1870
6	Deer	2330
7	Sheep	8220
8	Large 'chet' loaves	73,000
9	Small 'manchet' loaves	250,000
10	Gallons of ale	600,000

When did the first Indian restaurant open in Britain?

The honour should probably go to the Hindostanee Coffee House, which opened off Portman Square, London, in 1809. Its owner was a remarkable man called Dean Mahomet, who had arrived in London from India two years earlier. Mahomet's establishment offered, in the words of one of its advertisements, 'India dishes in the highest perfection', but, sadly, the public was not ready for them, and the Hindostanee Coffee House went bust in 1812. *Nick Rennison*

Visiting London recently, I passed a pub in Soho called The King of Corsica. Who was the King of Corsica?

The pub is named after an adventurer called Theodor von Neuhoff, who was born in Cologne in 1694. In the mid-18th century Neuhoff became involved in the Corsican struggle for independence from its then rulers in Genoa, and in 1736 he was proclaimed king of the island. His rule soon faltered, however, and he was obliged to flee a few months later. Neuhoff ended his days in London, where he died penniless in 1756. He was buried in St Ann's Church, Soho, and his grave, together with an epitaph written by Horace Walpole, can still be seen there. *Nick Rennison*

Several sources I have read mention medieval London's 16 conduits or public fountains. Can you tell me where they were?

For many centuries Londoners relied on natural streams to supply their water, but by the 13th century these were dangerously polluted. The solution was to pipe water from more distant streams to large stone conduits, where it could be stored and distributed to the city's inhabitants. The first to be built was the Great Conduit in West Cheap in the late 13th century. There followed a spate of others, and by the time of John Stow's *Survey of London* in 1598 there were more than 20. Two were situated at Oldbourne Cross and Bishopgate, and there was the Little Conduit at Stockes Market, known as 'the pissing conduit' because of the trickle of water it emitted. By the early 18th century many conduits had been ruined by the Great Fire or pulled down to make way for traffic. As newer forms of water conveyance took hold, the conduits gradually disappeared. *Rob Attar*

Why did rationing continue in Britain after the Second World War?

Food rationing was introduced in Britain on 8 January 1940, and lasted 14 years. What began as a wartime measure was extended into peacetime because of the desperate state of the British economy. In 1945 Britain was victorious but virtually bankrupt: 28 per cent of the national wealth had been lost, and British exports were severely reduced. In August of that year the US government ended its Lend-Lease scheme, which plunged the Labour government into a crisis. Reliant on loans from the USA and Canada to stay afloat, Britain endured a lengthy period of economic hardship. A wide 'dollar gap' opened, as Britain was critically short of US currency when dollars were desperately needed to buy vital American goods. Rationing was a facet of these years of austerity. Bread and potatoes, which had not been rationed during the war, came under rationing in 1946 and 1947 respectively. Towards the end of the decade Britain's financial position improved, in part through generous American provision of Marshall Aid, but also because of efficient management of the economy and the devaluation of the pound in 1949. Gradually, rationing ended – clothes rationing was abolished in 1949; petrol in 1950; and various foodstuffs from 1948 to 1953. The final items derationed were meat and bacon, on 4 July 1954 – a day of much rejoicing. *Gary Sheffield*

Why are there so many pubs in England called The Marquis of Granby? Who was the Marquis of Granby?

John Manners, Marquis of Granby, was an 18th-century soldier who fought in Scotland and Flanders before making his name during the Seven Years War. As commander of British forces in Europe, he won several victories against the French and their allies, and gained plaudits for his efforts at Minden in 1759, Warburg in 1760 and Gravenstein, Wilhelmstahl and Homburg in 1761. The fact that his name is still attached to pubs is a tribute to the popularity he once had. *Nick Rennison*

When was the last time anyone in Britain resorted to cannibalism to avoid starving?

Ireland was part of Britain at the time of the great famine in the mid-19th century, and that's the most likely answer. Hundreds of thousands starved to death between 1845 and 1851 (a similar famine affected the Scottish Highlands, though with less severe results), and you would expect several reports of cannibalism. In fact, there were very few, and these are mostly second-hand rumours – certainly nothing on the scale of reports of, for example, cannibalism in Russia in the 1920s and 1930s. Although English history features frequent food shortages, there have been no outright famines since 1623–4, thanks to a diversity of crops and the Poor Laws.

It's possible that there has been no cannibalism from necessity since the terrible famine that struck western Europe in 1315–17. English legal records do, however, feature occasional cases of mariners consuming their shipmates. The last famous case concerned three survivors of the barque *Mignonette* in 1884, who were in an open boat in the South Atlantic and consumed the cabin boy. On being rescued and returned to England, two of them were found guilty of murder at Exeter Assizes. There was an immediate appeal and retrial in which they were both convicted of manslaughter and each sentenced to six months. One lawyer allegedly remarked afterwards: 'Damn funny country we live in. Kill a cabin boy and you get six months. Bugger him and you get two years.' *Eugene Byrne*

When were chips (French fries) first thought of, and why served with fish?

Chips might have been invented in Spain, where the first potatoes arrived from the New World – there's even a claim that they were invented by St Teresa of Avila! Belgians claim that chips originated in their country, and the French tend to agree with them, even though one of the most authoritative early descriptions of chips comes from American statesman Thomas Jefferson, who said they were a French dish. The American belief in the Gallic origin led to the expression 'French fries'.

Fish and chips came together in Britain in the 19th century. The new trawling techniques of the North Sea fishing fleet made it profitable to catch large quantities of unfashionable species, which could now be rapidly transported to cities by rail before they went off, and sold cheaply to working-class consumers. The first recorded fish and chip shops appear in London and the north during the 1860s, the legend being that fish fryers would throw pieces of potato into the oil to cool it when it overheated, and would sell or even give away the resulting 'chips' to their customers. Early shops were usually family-run concerns based around a pot of oil on a coal-fired range, and they were often regarded as rather disreputable. The great Harry Ramsden, for instance, tried as a young man to escape the family business, and when he did return to it, his success was based on bringing it up-market. *Eugene Byrne*

I was surprised to read recently that George Bernard Shaw was a vegetarian. Were there many vegetarians in Shaw's time, and how did vegetarianism originate?

In Shaw's time (he died in 1950, aged 94) vegetarians were regarded by most people as mildly eccentric, but they were by no means unusual. Even during the Second World War, the government arranged extra supplies of cheese and/or nuts for the thousands of Britons who had no use for a meat ration. While most humans throughout history have been involuntary vegetarians most of the time, those who were vegetarian on principle have been around a long time as well. In ancient Greece, Pythagoras and his closest followers adhered to a strict vegetarian diet, and until the mid-19th century people who rejected meat were generally known as Pythagoreans. Famous Pythagoreans included Leonardo da Vinci,

Jean-Jacques Rousseau, Benjamin Franklin, Percy Bysshe Shelley, Richard Wagner and Leo Tolstoy. The main celebrity vegetarian of Shaw's time was Mahatma Gandhi. Adolf Hitler was put on a vegetarian diet by his doctors in the 1930s because of his stomach pains, but he occasionally ate ham and sausages, and certainly never promoted vegetarianism.

The modern vegetarian movement originated in Britain and the USA in the 19th century, its members being motivated by a range of beliefs – a vegetarian diet is healthier, killing animals is ethically wrong, meat-eating inflames sinful passions, etc. Many early proponents were evangelical Christians who saw abstinence from meat in similar terms to abstaining from alcohol. The term 'vegetarian' was first used in the 1840s with the foundation of the Vegetarian Society. Vegetarianism has been growing ever since. The society nowadays claims 3.5 million Britons are either vegetarian or vegan. *Eugene Byrne*

Reading about 18th-century London, I have come across many mentions of oysters being commonly eaten by ordinary people. When did they become a luxury food?

Some of mankind's earliest settlements were on seashores because of plentiful food supplies. Since oysters occur in tidal waters worldwide, they're one of the most ancient items in the human diet. They have also been farmed since (at least) Roman times, and became a cheap and common element of the working-class diet in many parts of Europe and North America well into the 19th century. 'Poverty and oysters always seem to go together,' said Sam Weller in Dickens's *Pickwick Papers*. But by the 19th century Britain's native beds were being over-exploited due to demand from rapidly expanding city populations. In some places, foreign varieties were introduced in an effort to make up the shortfall; these sometimes died of disease, or infected native strains. Other oyster beds were affected by newfangled sewage outlets, which polluted them, or smothered them in sediment. In a particularly notorious case, guests at a banquet in Winchester in 1902 contracted typhoid, and some, including the local bishop, died after eating sewage-contaminated oysters. Perhaps as Britain's seas and waterways become cleaner, sustainably cultivated oysters will make a big comeback rather than remaining an occasional indulgence. *Eugene Byrne*

How was it that French cuisine came to be recognised as the finest in Europe?

Louis XIV is a good starting-point. Meals were an integral part of the elaborate ceremony and display at the court of the Sun King, where everything had to be the very best. Louis was served soups, hors d'oeuvres, salads, roast dishes and desserts. It's surely no coincidence that, according to one theory, Louis' second wife, Madame de Maintenon, established the Cordon Bleu School. It is during this period that we also see the development of the sauces that were essential to so many dishes. The aristocracy and emerging middle classes emulated courtly tastes, while even comparatively modest families treated food with more care than most people in other countries. The French Revolution was crucial: it broke up restrictive catering guilds and aristocratic households, putting a small army of excellent cooks out on the streets. This led to a huge rise in the number of restaurants, and the start of a French tradition of dining out. At the same time, the chef Antoine Carême (1784–1833) became the most influential in the world. Carême, and later Auguste Escoffier (1846–1945), are regarded as the founders of haute cuisine, and not only laid down how food should be prepared and served, but also how kitchens should be organised. French chefs, and those trained in France, spread around the world, and they remain arbiters of culinary fashion. *Eugene Byrne*

In a book of old traditions I saw a reference to the Baddeley Cake. What is or was the Baddeley Cake?

Robert Baddeley was an 18th-century actor who was one of the cast in the original production of Richard Sheridan's play *The School for Scandal*. When he died in November 1794 he left property to found a home for 'decayed' actors, and also £3 per annum to provide wine and a specially baked cake in the green room of Drury Lane Theatre, London, every Twelfth Night. The ceremony of cutting (and eating) the Baddeley Cake has remained an annual tradition at the theatre. *Nick Rennison*

CHAPTER 7

RELIGION AND RITUAL, OR THE MYSTERY OF THE FATAL VESPERS

Who or what is 'Mephisto'?

Mephisto, or Mephistopheles, is a demon in Christian belief. His name occurs nowhere in the Bible, but seems to have emerged from medieval theology, probably in Germany. According to the most widespread stories, Mephisto was one of the angels closely beloved by God. During the creation of the Earth, Mephisto was in charge of the creation of sea mammals, and took the greatest delight in producing the orca, or killer whale. When God created humans and gave them dominion over all animals on Earth, Mephisto was annoyed that his orcas had been neglected by the Almighty. For this reason, Mephisto became the first angel to join the rebellion against God organised by Satan. The name Mephistopheles is Greek for 'He who shuns the light', and was probably devised to link this fallen angel to the darkness as opposed to the light of God's grace. His most famous role is as the demon sent to conclude the pact with Faust in the German folk tale. Faust promises to serve Satan in hell after his death in return for all he desires while alive on Earth. As death approaches, Faust tries to evade his fate by preaching God's love to the world, but in vain. His horribly mangled body is found one morning after Mephisto returns to claim Faust's soul. The story was later reworked into a book by Johann Goethe and an opera by Hector Berlioz, among many other versions. *Rupert Matthews*

Many devout Muslim women wear veils or burkas, but was there ever a Christian equivalent?

Islam calls for *hijab*, which in its widest sense means 'modesty or morality'. Muslim scholars have long debated what this should mean in practice. Tradition, as much as scriptural authority, calls for the wearing of anything from a simple headscarf to more comprehensive garments, such as a burka or jilbab. Christian teaching similarly emphasises that men and women should dress modestly, although – unless you count the nun's habit – this often only amounts to head coverings for women, particularly when attending religious services. This has sometimes been a requirement of Catholic canon law; it was also called for by reformers, such as John Calvin and Martin Luther, as well as being a practice in some Orthodox churches. Scarves or veils were widely worn by women until relatively recently, and are still common in some smaller Protestant denominations. A modern remnant of this practice is the mantilla, a lace veil usually worn by women when meeting the pope, though not all do so. Princess Diana wore one for her audience with the pontiff, but Irish President Mary Robinson did not. *Eugene Byrne*

In a book about the Gunpowder Plot I found a reference to 'The Fatal Vespers'. What was it?

On 5 November 1623 more than 300 people were gathered in an upstairs room in the French ambassador's house in London to take part in a religious service. The floor beams gave way and 95 people, including the two Jesuit priests conducting the service, were killed. The disaster, most often called 'The Fatal Vespers', was assumed by many Protestant Londoners to be God's judgement on Catholics for their idolatrous practices and involvement in the Gunpowder Plot, discovered exactly 18 years earlier. *Nick Rennison*

Who was the first pope and how was he elected?

There is no easy answer to this question, especially as there is a lack of clarity as to what the early popes were. The pope, as we understand it today, is the Bishop of Rome and head of the Roman Catholic Church, but at the dawn of Christianity there was no clear hierarchy in place. Many Catholics consider St Peter to have been the first pope, but it is hard to find evidence of a clear line from Peter onwards. In AD 180 the Christian writer Iranaeus devised the first surviving list of popes, which began with Linus, thought to have become pope in AD 67. But these lists are retrospective and unreliable – for example, the sixth name in Iranaeus's list is Sextus, which translates as 'the sixth'. As for how the earliest popes were chosen, again we simply don't know, although it was most likely via some process of election by the Christian communities in Rome. The first pope to be chosen by the current system – election by the College of Cardinals – was Celestine IV in 1241. *Rob Attar*

During the Reformation and Dissolution, a great number of England's stained-glass windows were destroyed. What happened to all the broken glass?

During the Reformation, the more ardent Protestants objected to religious imagery of any kind. Wall paintings were whitewashed over, statues were toppled, and the vast majority of stained-glass windows, which had previously adorned practically every religious building in the land, were smashed or removed. Attempts were made to sell the glass as scrap, but the mid-16th century was a time of upheaval in the glass industry. New techniques of making clear, thin glass were sweeping Europe. The glass from most churches was coloured and could not be blown into the new thin-sided forms. A few craftsmen were able to reuse the old coloured glass in new windows depicting armorial bearings for the gentry, but most of it was melted down to produce crude and clumsy vessels for the poorer members of society. These items did not last long, and hardly any now survive. In brief, the broken glass ended up on the nearest dump in a very short space of time. *Rupert Matthews*

Is it true that a 19th-century religious group actually predicted the end of the world in August 1914?

Many religious sects in the 19th century claimed to know the date of Armageddon. In the 1870s Charles Taze Russell, founder of the Watchtower Society, predicted the world's end in 1914. He didn't specify the month, and was expecting something more apocalyptic than the First World War. He later revised the date. *Nick Rennison*

Did 50,000 children really go on crusade in 1212?

Very unlikely. The standard account has it that in France a teenage lad named Stephen of Cloyes raised around 30,000 young followers, while a boy called Nicholas got about 20,000 German children to follow him. The plan was to travel to Jerusalem, where the infidels would bow down before their pious innocence. The French party travelled to Marseilles and were offered free passage to the Holy Land, but were sold into slavery in North Africa instead. The German group's numbers were depleted crossing the Alps, and when they reached Rome, Pope Innocent III told them to go home and grow up. This, though, is a conflation of various mentions of a 'children's crusade' all dating from well after the time it supposedly happened. If 30,000 under-age zealots really had turned up in Marseilles, it would have been noted as a miracle by several chroniclers at the time.

In France there were many landless young men wandering the countryside, and the historian Georges Duby suggested that the word used to describe the child crusaders – *pueri*, the Latin for 'boys' – at that time actually denoted young men of the lower classes.

It could be that the whole idea of a children's crusade is based upon a misinterpretation. *Eugene Byrne*

In London there is a street called Crutched Friars. Who were the Crutched Friars?

The Friars of the Holy Cross were an order of mendicant monks who established a religious house in London in the mid-13th century. The name 'Crutched Friars' has no connection with the word 'crutch' in the sense of a wooden staff, but comes from a corruption of the Latin *crux*, meaning 'cross'. *Nick Rennison*

Did you know...?

In the medieval period 18 churches across Europe claimed to possess the Holy Foreskin that had been removed from Jesus Christ during His circumcision. Since Christ ascended to heaven, the only body parts available for veneration were those removed prior to his Ascension, including his foreskin. *Nick Rennison*

Did medieval theologians ever really debate how many angels you could fit on to the head of a pin?

Not as far as we know – this is actually a caricature put about in later centuries. The earliest known references to angels and needles (not pins) are from 17th-century English theologians Joseph Glanvill and Ralph Cudworth. The latter, in his book *The True Intellectual System of the Universe* (1678), says: 'Some who are far from atheists, may make themselves merry with that conceit of thousands of spirits dancing at once upon a needle's point.' Cudworth seems to be referring to a facetious intellectual game that almost certainly derives from St Thomas Aquinas's 13th-century work *Summa Theologica*, which set out Catholic dogma and attempted to reconcile faith and reason. Aquinas made a number of tortured propositions about angels: 'Is an angel's movement in time or instantaneous? In passing from place to place, does he pass through intervening space?' So while Aquinas didn't talk about angels on needles, he came pretty close to it.

The fictitious 'debate' was popularised by Isaac D'Israeli (1766–1848, father of prime minister Benjamin), who published some best-selling books of historical curiosities. 'The reader desirous of being merry with Aquinas's angels,' he wrote, 'may find them in Martinus Scriblerus, in ch VII who inquires if angels pass from one extreme to another without going through the middle? And if angels know things more clearly in a morning? How many angels can dance on the point of a very fine needle, without jostling one another?' 'Martinus Scriblerus' was an 18th-century Tory satirical collective that included Jonathan Swift, Alexander Pope, John Gay and others, who did indeed lampoon Aquinas and his angels, but did not mention needles or pins. That was D'Israeli's own addition. *Eugene Byrne*

What happened to the monks and nuns thrown out by Henry VIII's Dissolution of the Monasteries?

It is not generally recognised that relatively small numbers of clerics were affected by Henry's closure of English monasteries in the 1530s. Many monasteries had fewer than a dozen monks or nuns in residence, and even the largest had barely 50. In 1536, when the Dissolution began, there were probably only some 12,000 monks and nuns, and the number was declining rapidly. Aware that the closure of the monasteries would not be universally popular, Henry VIII went out of his way to appease the critics. Although most of the land went to the government, some was handed over to the Court of Augmentations. This body funded many schools and colleges to replace the educational work of the religious houses. It also paid pensions to the monks and nuns who had been evicted from their homes. These pensions were generous enough to provide a modest rural lifestyle, although, as with so many government payments then and since, they were often paid in arrears. Only a few of the monks opposed the closure of their religious houses so forcefully that violence had to be used. Most accepted the pensions offered and lived quietly for the rest of their lives; some were even granted chambers on or near their old homes. One abbot in Shropshire actually bought his old monastic lands, announced he was now a Protestant and lived out his life in the role of local squire. *Rupert Matthews*

Who is the youngest person ever to become pope?

Because records of the early Church are not always reliable, this is a difficult question to answer with certainty, but the youngest pope was probably John XII, the son of a Roman nobleman, who was elected pontiff in 955 at the age of 18. He sat on the throne of St Peter for eight and a half years, but didn't prove much of an ornament to it. John XII was renowned for his womanising, and he might well have been killed by the husband of one of the many women he bedded. *Nick Rennison*

When people thought the world was flat, what did they imagine the underneath to look like?

The curious thing is that the majority of the world's population never did think the world was flat. There is evidence that our ancestors were well aware of the world's spherical nature. Aristotle noted it in the 4th century BC, for example, as did Ptolemy around AD 150. It was only in the last 200 years that people began to presume belief in a flat earth was ever widespread. The American author Washington Irving helped create this myth in 1828 by producing a rather unhistorical biography of Christopher Columbus, which depicted the explorer challenging his 'ignorant' Christian contemporaries about the shape of the world. The story was then propagated by science writers later in the 19th century, aiming to discredit religion by showing it to be a permanent enemy of rational science. The error crept into textbooks and common lore, and now, despite the idea being discredited by historians of science, it has proved difficult to replace. This is not to say that nobody has ever believed the world to be flat, and indeed a Flat Earth Society exists today. There has rarely been consensus as to what is underneath, but you can take your pick from an enormous tortoise, a giant boar or simply nothing at all. *Rob Attar*

Did King Henry VIII's Dissolution of the Monasteries affect the monasteries of Scotland, in particular Jedburgh Abbey?

The magnificent ruins of Jedburgh Abbey are among the most impressive monastic ruins anywhere in Britain. The Augustinian abbey was founded around 1138, and ten years later King David I donated money and lands that made the establishment wealthy enough to begin construction of the mighty church that still dominates the town of Jedburgh today. The ruined condition of Jedburgh Abbey is not, however, the result of Henry VIII's Dissolution of the Monasteries in the 1530s. Henry was King of England, and Jedburgh lies in Scotland, which was then entirely independent of England under the rule of King James V. But it was Henry VIII of England who had a hand in the ruination of Jedburgh. He strongly disapproved of the alliance between James and France. Border warfare was fierce during the early 16th century. Jedburgh was attacked in 1523 and again in 1544. The abbey was gutted by fire, and no attempt was made to rebuild it due to the turmoil of wars with England and the religious reformation. *Rupert Matthews*

In 1290 Edward I expelled all of England's Jews. Have any other groups ever been expelled from Britain?

Being an island, Britain has not tended to have minority populations from another nation. As a result, mass expulsions have not been as frequent as in other European states. Indeed, the expulsion of the Jews in 1290, following decades of ill feeling and occasional persecution, is unique. The closest event was the notorious St Brice's Day Massacre of 1002, the details of which are rather obscure. The orders were given by King Ethelred II – not without reason known as 'the Unready' or 'badly advised' – on the advice of a nobleman named Hunna, who claimed to have uncovered a Danish plot to assassinate Ethelred. Orders to round up and kill all Danes were distributed to local officials, with St Brice's Day (13 November) fixed as the day of action. How widely the orders were obeyed it is impossible to know, and in any case, they probably did not extend to the Danelaw of northern and eastern England, where large numbers of people of Danish extraction had been living for generations. The most notorious incident took place in Oxford, when a group of Danes

Did you know...?

The last man to be condemned to death by the Spanish Inquisition was a village schoolmaster named Cayetano Ripoll. Accused of being a deist and a Freemason, Ripoll was garrotted in a square in Valencia in July 1826. *Nick Rennison*

sought sanctuary in St Frideswide's Church. The church was burnt down, killing everyone within.

Ethelred was probably emboldened to act after securing an alliance with the Normans following his marriage to Emma, daughter of Richard, Duke of Normandy, earlier that year. If Ethelred hoped the killings and expulsions would ensure peace, he was wrong. Among the dead were a lady named Gunnhilde and her children. Gunnhilde was sister to King Svein Forkbeard of Denmark, who promptly raised an army and fleet with which to invade England and wreak vengeance. England would know no peace for the rest of Ethelred's lifetime. *Rupert Matthews*

Does Witchfinder General Matthew Hopkins deserve his evil reputation?

Possibly not. The process of condemning Hopkins as a depraved impostor began even before his death in 1647. At the Restoration he was lumped in with the regicides, and by 1700 reviled as a bloodthirsty and paranoid inquisitor. Today, in an age sensitive to past injustice, 'witches' are viewed as innocent victims, and their persecutors as ignorant or evil. Yet 'evil' is not a useful historical category because it explains away puzzling and distressing facts, serving only to express emotion. This is why the tabloids like it.

After publication of his biography of Hitler, Ian Kershaw was criticised for refusing to condemn his subject as 'evil'. His defence was that he was striving only to understand. Some might protest that to understand all is to forgive all, but historians are not in the business of forgiving or condemning: their job is to tell the truth, however complex, nuanced and troubling. Hopkins lived at a time when witchcraft was a capital crime, belief in satanic agency universal, and righteous anger about the political and spiritual future of England intense. Like many godly warriors in the 1640s, he believed he was fighting Armageddon. He did not accuse

111

anyone; rather he helped others make accusations that they might have been reluctant to make given the high acquittal rate for witchcraft. His career would not have been possible without the enthusiastic participation of hundreds of people, from witnesses and midwives to magistrates and judges. If he was evil, then they must share his guilt. *Malcolm Gaskill*

Is it true that Charles Darwin and his theory of evolution single-handedly destroyed the almost universal religious faith people had until then?

Arguments around evolutionary theory tell us as much about our own age as they do about the Victorians. Evolution is now the battleground in the conflict between most scientists on one side and 'creationists' (usually biblical literalists) plus adherents of 'intelligent design' on the other. But the historic forces undermining universal faith were in place well before the 1859 publication of *On the Origin of Species*. The Reformation took interpretation of scripture from the control of religious authority and allowed anyone to read and study the Bible. The Enlightenment and the rise of science then led to the examination and exposure of its inconsistencies. The treatment of the Bible as history rather than the word of God was arguably as important to the decline of universal faith as Darwinism. There are probably several other factors as well, such as the decline of traditional communities and peer pressure to attend church, or improvements in medical science. But the list is potentially endless and charged with all sorts of theological and political controversy. Surveys suggest that around 10–15 per cent of the UK population now regularly attends religious services, Christian or otherwise. However, only 15.5 per cent of respondents said they had 'no religion' in the 2001 census, and the proportion of actual atheists is probably lower. Darwin and the Enlightenment did not turn us all into non-believers – they turned most of us into agnostics and occasional churchgoers. *Eugene Byrne*

What are the origins of the birthday bumps?

Probably the Reformation, as before then birthdays were hardly ever celebrated. In Catholic societies the feast day of the saint you were named after was more cause for celebration than the anniversary of your birth. According to Iona and Peter Opie's

1959 classic *The Lore and Language of Schoolchildren*, there was a wide regional variation in British birthday rituals 50 years ago, including pinching, hair-pulling, slapping and the bumps (known as 'the dumps' in parts of Scotland). From other sources it's also plain that violent birthday ordeals were common throughout the Anglo-Saxon world, though they now seem to be in decline. What is noticeable is that almost all involve a slap, kick, tug or bump for the number of years the victim is celebrating, and then, almost inevitably, one or more extra 'for luck'. The Opies note a mention of bumping as a treatment for bullies in the 18th century, and of course tossing people in a blanket has been a form of humiliation since the Greeks and Romans, if not earlier. Bumping is also very redolent of the medieval Catholic custom of ritual hitting on important occasions. The idea was that illiterate people would recall, say, witnessing a marriage or contract by remembering the clout they had endured. *Eugene Byrne*

10 Archbishops who died violently

Ten high-ranking holy men who didn't go in peace.

1 **Aelfeah** (Canterbury) beaten to death by Danes, 1012

2 **Thomas Becket** (Canterbury) murdered in Canterbury Cathedral, 1170

3 **Simon of Sudbury** (Canterbury) head hacked off during Peasants' Revolt, 1381

4 **Richard Scrope** (York) beheaded for treason, 1403

5 **John Alen** (Dublin) murdered near Clontarf, 1534

6 **David Beaton** (St Andrews) murdered in his castle, 1546

7 **Thomas Cranmer** (Canterbury) burnt for heresy, 1556

8 **John Hamilton** (St Andrews) hanged for complicity in murder, 1571

9 **William Laud** (Canterbury) beheaded for treason, 1645

10 **Oliver Plunkett** (Armagh) hanged, drawn and quartered for treason, 1681

How far back in history does 'jumping the brush' go as a substitute marriage ceremony?

In Britain it goes back at least as far as the 18th century, and probably a lot earlier than that. We know it was used by itinerant working people, such as sailors or canal-digging 'navvies' who couldn't afford a church wedding (or didn't have access to a church), but wanted to legitimise their relationship in the eyes of family and friends. Among seamen, it was occasionally the case that two or more sailors would jump the brush with the same woman to whom they would then remit their pay for safekeeping. To this day some people still use 'living over the brush' as an expression for a cohabiting unmarried couple.

'Jumping the broom' became a common ceremony among slaves in early 19th-century America, who had no legal right to marry. Some historians claim that it comes from some ancient West African ritual, while others say it's a wholly African-American invention, but you have to suspect that the idea might actually have come from working-class Britons. You can speculate on the brush 'sweeping away' evil spirits, or as a fertility symbol (handle, bushy bit, etc.), but surely the simplest explanation is that the brush is an obvious symbol of domesticity. Some modern African-American weddings follow the tradition, although many people deplore it precisely because of its slave-era connotations. It's also increasingly popular among modern pagans, whose 'handfasting' partnership ceremonies often incorporate broom-jumping on the basis that the broom is supposedly a fertility symbol in Celtic mythology. *Eugene Byrne*

I've heard about a medieval king who wanted to make England an Islamic nation. Who was the king and what were the circumstances behind his wish to change the country's religion?

The monarch in question was King John (r. 1199–1216). In 1205 Hubert Walter, the Archbishop of Canterbury, died. At this period there were three claimants to the right to choose a successor. John claimed it as King of England; the English bishops claimed it on behalf of the clergy; and the monks of Canterbury claimed it as the archbishop was also their abbot. Usually, the three would squabble and bargain until they agreed on a candidate. This time, however, the Canterbury monks appealed to Pope Innocent III to decide who was in the right. Innocent sided with the monks, then used his authority as pope to order them to appoint his friend Stephen Langton. When John discovered what had happened he fell into a violent temper that was spectacular even by the standards of this dangerously ill-tempered monarch. He damned Innocent to hell, threatened to blind the papal envoys and promised to slit Langton's nose if he ever came to Canterbury. John then moved quickly to confiscate papal lands, seize papal assets and expel all the pope's friends from England. According to the chronicler Matthew Paris, writing shortly afterwards, it was at this time that John wrote to Muhammad An-Nâsir, a powerful Saracen ruler based in Egypt, promising that he would make England a Muslim country if An-Nâsir would make war on the pope. Given John's temper, it is not unlikely that he made such a promise, though there is no proof that he actually did. Other sources name different Muslim rulers as the recipients of John's promise, and date the letter a few years later. Pope Innocent responded by excommunicating John and putting all of England under interdict, meaning that of all church services, only baptisms, weddings and funerals could be held, and those only in the church yard. The dispute dragged on until 1213, when John finally backed down. *Rupert Matthews*

In the film *Mrs Brown*, after the recovery of the Prince of Wales from typhoid, the queen ordered that 'a Mass' should be said in thanksgiving. Surely the very Protestant Queen Victoria would have done no such thing?

When the future King Edward VII fell ill with typhoid in the winter of 1871 the disease assumed great personal and constitutional importance for his mother, Queen Victoria. Victoria's beloved husband Prince Albert had died from typhoid in 1861 following a visit to the youthful Edward at Cambridge, where he had admonished him for becoming embroiled in a scandal with an actress. Victoria partly blamed Edward for Albert's death, and the relationship between mother and son became strained. She effectively retired from public life as a widow, encouraging republican sentiment to grow among a sizeable minority of the population. Republicanism was boosted in the summer of 1870 when Emperor Napoleon III was ousted from France and a republic established.

Prince Edward's growing popularity made his near-fatal illness a matter of public concern, and his recovery from the disease effectively marked the end of the rise in republicanism in Britain. His mother was greatly relieved not to lose another family member to typhoid, and was reconciled to her wayward son. Given the private and public importance of Edward's recovery, it is hardly surprising that Victoria used her position as head of the Church of England to order that a thanksgiving service should be held. That Protestant service included in it a Holy Communion as set out in the Book of Common Prayer. Some Catholic congregations also held thanksgiving services, which included a Mass, and it is this that may have led to some confusion. At this time Catholics had only recently achieved full civic rights under English law, and it was felt that it would be diplomatic to hold such services, though Victoria had neither ordered them nor, of course, had the power to do so.
Rupert Matthews

CHAPTER 8

POLITICS,
OR
THE ABSENT QUEEN

According to a famous footnote by A.J.P. Taylor in his *English History 1914–45*, King George V had his trousers creased at the sides, not the front and back. Is there any significance in this?

It's a peculiarity also remarked upon by Robert Graves and Alan Hodge in their wonderful, gossipy social history of the inter-war years, *The Long Weekend*. But if you see any pictures of George out of naval uniform, you find that, where you can make out any crease at all, it's definitely front and back. Of course, these are all photos of him at public occasions, so perhaps we should take the historians at their word and assume George wore his side-creases only in private.

The fashion for pressing trousers came in during the late 19th century. Some say it was the work of that great leader of fashion, King Edward VII – George's father – while he was still Prince of Wales. By the 1920s, with trousers getting baggier, a front-and-back crease was considered essential to preserve the line. In the Royal Navy, however, regulations stated that bell-bottom trousers were to be creased vertically along the seams. George V was a man whose character had been moulded by his time in the navy, turning him into a stickler for detail. We know of several instances of his criticising his sons' clothing in childhood (and later); the only forms of dress he considered acceptable for boys were kilts and the sailor suits that were miniaturised versions of the uniforms worn by lower-ranking members of the navy. It's possible that we got the idea of George considering side-creasing essential from one of his pronouncements on bell-bottoms and the correct creasing thereof. *Eugene Byrne*

Who was the Downing who gave his name to Downing Street?

Born in Dublin and brought up in America (he was one of the early graduates of Harvard University), Sir George Downing (1623–84) was a soldier, diplomat and politician who served first Oliver Cromwell and then, after the Restoration, Charles II. According to the diarist Samuel Pepys, Downing was 'a perfidious rogue' and certainly it seems he was only too willing to swap sides when it suited him. One of his rewards for supporting Charles was the land on which he built the street that now bears his name. *Nick Rennison*

Did the French have a national anthem before 'La Marseillaise', and, if so, what was it?

'La Marseillaise' was officially adopted as France's first national anthem in 1795, during the Revolution, but it fell out of favour under Napoleon. It was re-established as the anthem in 1879. In the intervening years there was no national anthem in the sense that we understand the term, although there were songs that had an unofficial status as national airs. Under Napoleon III, for example, a song entitled 'Partant pour la Syrie', composed by the emperor's mother, was so popular and played so regularly on state occasions that it was often thought of as the national anthem. *Nick Rennison*

10 Kings of England who aren't buried at Westminster or Windsor

None of these monarchs is interred where you might expect.

1 **William I**
Abbaye de St Stephen, Caen (d 1087)

2 **William II**
Winchester Cathedral (d 1100)

3 **Henry I**
Reading Abbey (d 1135)

4 **Henry II**
Fontevrault Abbey, France (d 1189)

5 **John**
Worcester Cathedral (d 1216)

6 **Edward II**
Gloucester Cathedral (d 1327)

7 **Henry IV**
Canterbury Cathedral (d 1413)

8 **Richard III**
Somewhere in Leicester (d 1485)

9 **James II**
St Germain-en-Laye, France (d 1701)

10 **George I**
Hanover, Germany (d 1727)

Did you know...?

The White House, the official home of the US President, was once burnt to the ground by British troops. In 1814, during the three-year war between the United States and Britain, soldiers from the United Kingdom and their Canadian allies briefly occupied Washington and set the building ablaze. *Nick Rennison*

Which monarch in history had the longest reign?

Queen Victoria ruled for 64 years. Franz Josef was emperor of Austria from 1848 to 1916, a total of 68 years. However, they are both outstripped by the Egyptian pharaoh Pepi II, who, according to some Egyptologists, ruled for 94 years in the 3rd millennium BC, from the age of six until his death as a centenarian. *Nick Rennison*

Recently I heard mention of King Louis of England. Could you give me some information on the elusive monarch?

In 1199 John became King of England. He made peace with France and married Isabella of Angoulême the next year. But it was a truce rather than peace. The war had started again in 1202, and by 1206 John had lost Anjou, Brittany, Maine and Normandy. An uneasy peace followed, but the war was renewed in 1213, with a brief pause in 1214. The English throne was weak, and in 1215, after the Concord of Runnymede, based on Magna Carta, had broken down, the first Barons' War started. The dauphin Louis (1187–1226, later King of France, 1223–6) saw his opportunity to claim the English throne and invade. In 1216 John died and the youth Henry III was crowned. He and his regents, led by William the Marshal, had title but not full control of the realm: the rebellious barons and Louis controlled half of England, including London. However, the animosities towards the late king had not translated to Henry. Thus, although Louis held castles of the south and east and the Channel (but not Dover), his authority did not always extend beyond those garrisons. Louis allowed his forces to be split, and so made it easier for their defeat at Lincoln. The barons went back to the English Crown, and his naval forces were defeated off Sandwich. Eventually, Louis was forced to sue for peace and was paid a handsome sum to quit England, doing so after the Treaty of Kingston-upon-Thames in 1217. *Christopher Lee*

Did you know…?

Suite 212 at Claridge's Hotel in London was temporarily ceded to Yugoslavia in 1945. On the orders of Winston Churchill, the rooms were declared Yugoslav territory for a day so that the baby born there to the exiled Queen of Yugoslavia could be said to have been born on Yugoslav soil. *Nick Rennison*

How many Welsh princes have actually ruled all of Wales?

Over the years there have been many princes in Wales, but only one was the undisputed ruler of all of modern-day Wales: Gruffydd ap Llywelyn. After the Romans left, the people who would become the Welsh were divided into a number of states, each ruled by a prince. The states were prone to division and collapse as competing nobles fought each other. In 1039 the ruler of Gwynedd died. His throne was seized by Gruffydd ap Llywelyn, a son of the previous prince, who came with a band of tough retainers to claim his inheritance. Later that year Gruffydd arranged the death of Prince Iago of Powys, then seized that state as well. The following years saw a campaign of intrigue, murder and outright warfare that gradually ousted all the princes in Wales, allowing Gruffydd to unite their lands. In 1057 the last independent ruler, Cadwgan of Glamorgan, fled. With Wales now united under his command, Gruffydd invaded England, torching Hereford and seizing border lands. However, in 1063 an English army drove Gruffydd back, deep into North Wales, where he was murdered by the avenging son of Prince Iago of Powys. Once again, Wales fell apart as the various princely families reasserted their petty states. Powerful Welsh princes would arise in the future, but none could unite all of Wales for much of it was by then under direct rule from England. *Rupert Matthews*

Is it true that the American flag, the Stars and Stripes, derives from the coat of arms of the Washington family?

The coat of arms does include stripes, but its 'stars' are in fact molets, the rowels on a rider's spur. The designer of the flag, a congressman called Francis Hopkinson, probably did not intend any reference to the Washington family coat of arms. *Nick Rennison*

Did Hitler ever visit England?

There has long been a story that Adolf Hitler visited Liverpool before the First World War to stay with his half-brother Alois. (The rumour provides the basis for Beryl Bainbridge's novel *Young Adolf*.) Alois certainly lived in Liverpool at the time, but the only evidence of his half-brother visiting him is a statement (in a memoir written during the Second World War) by Alois's Irish wife, Bridget. Her account is dismissed as an invention by most historians. *Nick Rennison*

What do the five stars on the Chinese national flag stand for?

The current national flag of China dates back to 1 October 1949. That was the day on which the People's Republic of China was officially brought into being. The Communists wanted a new flag for their new regime and launched a nationwide competition for a design. Of the 3000 or so entries received, a committee of leading Communists chose the current design for its simplicity and symbolism.

The red field stands for the Communist revolution, but is also symbolic of good luck in Chinese tradition. The large star symbolises the guiding role of the Communist Party, while the four smaller stars are said to represent the essential unity of the Chinese people under the Party. The stars were coloured gold to symbolise the dawn of a new era of hope under Communism.

The design was put forward by Zeng Liansong, the secretary of the Shanghai Modern Economics Agency. He was invited to Beijing to watch the first official flying of the flag, hoisted by Mao Zedong in front of a crowd of 300,000. Every dawn the official flag is hoisted over Tiananmen Square in a ceremony lasting precisely two minutes and seven seconds, the time it takes for the sun to rise over the city. *Rupert Matthews*

Wish I hadn't said that...

'We're all right! We're all right!'
Labour leader Neil Kinnock at a televised election rally, eight days before the Conservatives won their fourth general election victory in a row, April 1992.

Recently I read that before 1939 Winston Churchill was one of the least trusted politicians in Britain. Why was this, and how did his reputation change so dramatically for the better?

Churchill alienated a number of groups in his long political career. Many Tories distrusted him because he defected to the Liberals before the First World War. His exclusion from major office was one of the conditions of the Tories joining the wartime coalition in 1915. Even after he rejoined the Conservatives in the 1920s, Churchill was distrusted by many party members, and Stanley Baldwin and Neville Chamberlain kept him out of the government in the 1930s. The Labour movement remembered Churchill's bellicosity against the workers when he was Liberal Home Secretary and later during the General Strike of 1926. The 1915 Gallipoli fiasco, Churchill's intemperate opposition to Dominion status for India in the 1930s, and his quixotic support for King Edward VIII during the abdication crisis all called his judgement into question. The rise of Hitler changed Churchill's life. Although he was neither as consistent nor as prescient as he would later claim, Churchill's warnings against appeasement caused his stock to rise. By the time he re-entered the government on the outbreak of war in September 1939, many were prepared to set aside their doubts because they recognised his talent for war. His subsequent performance as prime minister from May 1940 onwards confirmed this view. *Gary Sheffield*

Is it true that Captain Bligh, years after the mutiny on the *Bounty*, was the victim of another mutiny by men he commanded?

In 1808, nearly 20 years after the mutiny on the *Bounty*, Bligh was governor of New South Wales in Australia. Soldiers there rebelled against his authority, arrested him and took control of the colony. The British government was obliged to send out a new governor to replace Bligh. *Nick Rennison*

Why does the Hawaiian state flag have a Union Jack on it?

The Hawaiian flag consists of a field of red, blue and white horizontal bars, with a Union Jack in the upper left canton, where the white stars on a blue field appear on the USA flag. The reasons for this are to be found in the history of the island chain.

While there is archaeological evidence suggesting habitation as early as *c*. AD 300, the islands were certainly settled by Polynesians over 1000 years ago, and discovered by Europeans in 1778 when Captain Cook arrived. The islands were united in 1810 by King Kamehameha of Hawaii Island, with a British seaman named Isaac Davis acting as his army commander. British naval and trading ships were frequent visitors in the decades that followed, and in 1843 the Royal Navy briefly occupied Hawaii. By the 1880s the economy of the islands was dominated by American links. In 1893 a group of American businessmen, aided by US sailors, mounted a coup that overthrew Queen Liliuokalani. Bloodshed and rioting followed, and in 1898 the USA annexed the islands. The inclusion of the Union Jack in the Hawaiian state flag was a tribute to the British discovery of the islands and British involvement in their 18th- and early 19th-century history. *Rupert Matthews*

10 Famous riots

And the reasons people took to the streets in protest.

1 **Oxford**
(February 1355) town–gown enmity

2 **London**
(May 1517) a violent protest against foreigners

3 **Hexham, Northumberland**
(March 1761) opposition to conscription into the militia

4 **London**
(June 1780) anti-Catholicism stirred up by Lord George Gordon

5 **Bristol**
(September 1793) introduction of toll on Bristol Bridge

6 **Littleport, Cambridgeshire**
(1816) economic distress

7 **Bristol**
(1831) House of Lords' rejection of Reform Act on the electoral system

8 **Newport**
(1839) confrontation between Chartists and authorities

9 **Basingstoke**
(1880) arrival of the Salvation Army in the town

10 **Tonypandy**
(1910) unrest during miners' strike

Which current country has kept its name the longest?

Some countries have been known rather loosely by the same name for a very great period of time. Both Italy and Spain have been known by versions of those names for about 2500 years. However, neither was a united country until comparatively recently, and their current official names are even newer. Italy became the Repubblica Italiana in 1946, and Spain became the Reino de España in 1975. Japan has called itself Nippon since around AD 650. However, the boundaries of Japan have varied considerably over the years. There are two countries that compete to have the oldest name and boundaries. La Serenissima Repubblica di San Marino was founded as a self-governing monastery by the stonemason St Marino in around AD 300. However, it did not acquire independence as a republic until some time in the 13th century, and its boundaries were fixed soon after. Rather more certain are the origins of the Principat d'Andorra, which was founded within its current boundaries in 1278 by a treaty between the Bishop of Urgell and the Comte de Foix, who agreed to share the sovereignty of the place jointly. The rights of the Comte de Foix passed by inheritance to the kings of France and thus to the French Republic. Since France is now part of the European Union, the status of Andorra as a truly independent country is open to dispute. *Rupert Matthews*

Why was the swastika adopted by the Nazis?

The swastika is an ancient symbol, common to many cultures and sacred to Hindus, Jainists and Buddhists. Its use in modern Europe actually predates the Nazis. It was used in the United Kingdom, for instance, as an early device for the scouting movement, and in Finland was a traditional military emblem. Elsewhere it was seen as

Did you know...?

Pitcairn Island gave women the vote in 1838. In a constitution for the island that came into force that year, all adult women were allowed to vote. This was more than 50 years before New Zealand became the first self-governing nation to grant partial female suffrage in 1893. *Nick Rennison*

Did you know...?

Sir Isaac Newton served as an MP for a year in 1689–90 and then again in 1701-2. His only recorded contribution to parliamentary debate during his first spell was a request that a draughty window should be closed. *Nick Rennison*

a symbol of good luck, or a representation of the rising sun. It was first used in Germany in the early 20th century among the various radical nationalist sects, where its Indo-European origin was thought to symbolise the supposed dominance and purity of the 'Aryan' race – considered by some German nationalists to be the ancestors of the Germanic people. In this context, the swastika was used by – amongst others – the mystical-nationalist Thule Society and the Ehrhardt Brigade of the Freikorps long before the Nazi Party was established. As the Nazi Party grew largely out of that same cultural and intellectual milieu, it naturally inherited much of the same imagery. According to his autobiography *Mein Kampf*, Hitler personally authorised the adoption of the swastika, which he saw as a symbol of his party's mission – 'the victory of Aryan mankind'. The final design of the Nazi flag was made by a Munich dentist – one Friedrich Krone (who was also a member of the Thule Society). It was adopted as the German national flag in 1935 and was abolished following the collapse of the Nazi regime a decade later. *Roger Moorhouse*

Why was Tasmania originally called Van Diemen's Land, and why did the name change?

When the Dutch explorer Abel Tasman became the first European to sight the island in 1642, he thought he had discovered a vast new territory and he named it after his patron, Anthony van Diemen, the governor of the Dutch East Indies. The name was in use throughout the period when Britain transported its convicts down under. In fact, Van Diemen's Land became so linked in the public's mind with crime and transportation that, after it achieved a new status as a self-governing colony in 1825, it was given a new name that had none of the unfortunate associations of the old. *Nick Rennison*

10 Nicknames of Viking leaders

The epithets that had enemies trembling in their boots – with fear or laughter.

1 **Ragnar Hairy Breeches**
Viking chieftain, died c.850s

2 **Ivar the Boneless**
King of Dublin, died 870s

3 **Sigurd the Mighty**
Earl of Orkney, died late 9th century

4 **Erik Bloodaxe**
King of York, died 954

5 **Gorm the Old**
King of Denmark, died 959

6 **Thorfinn Skull-Splitter**
Earl of Orkney, died 963

7 **Svein Forkbeard**
King of Denmark, died 1014

8 **Einar Falsemouth**
Earl of Orkney, died 1020

9 **Harald the Ruthless**
King of Norway, died 1066

10 **Magnus Barelegs**
King of Norway, died 1103

In a recent programme on George, Duke of Kent, it was suggested that when Edward VIII abdicated, the duke might have been better suited to succeed to the throne than his brothers. Are the rules of succession after an abdication different from those after the death of the monarch?

Throughout most of Britain's history the succession to any of the various kingdoms and principalities was governed simply by custom and practice. This was a flexible system, allowing for changes as the need arose. However, by 1701 the then king, William III, was clearly dying. He had no children, nor did the next heir, the Princess Anne. By the custom then in place, there would be little choice but to invite back to the throne the ousted King James II. James had been thrown out in the 'Glorious Revolution' of 1688 on the grounds of his arrogance, incompetence and Catholicism. Although he had his supporters, most people did not want him back, so some legal mechanism had to be found to block his return. The result was the 1701 Act of Settlement. The main provision of the Act was to declare Sophia, Electress of Hanover and a granddaughter of Britain's King James I, as the heir after Princess Anne. Thereafter, the line of succession was to follow the heirs of Sophia. At the same time the Act established male primogeniture in law for the first time; previously, it had been merely a custom. James had been bypassed. The Act also said that no monarch could be a Catholic or married to one.

All these laws apply to the succession, whatever the reasons for a vacancy on the throne. Whether the previous monarch made way by death or abdication makes no difference to the law. There have been attempts over the years to alter the rules of succession. Most recently Lord Dubs introduced a Bill to Parliament in 2004 that would have ended male primogeniture, allowing the eldest child to succeed regardless of their gender. The Bill failed. As for the Duke of Kent, he might have been capable, but it is generally agreed that King George VI did a good job as monarch. *Rupert Matthews*

Did you know...?

Abraham Lincoln's Gettysburg Address on 19 November 1863 was only a two-minute addendum to the main speech made at Gettysburg that day. An almost forgotten two-hour-long speech by a politician named Edward Everett preceded it. *Nick Rennison*

Is it true that there was a queen of England who never once set foot in England?

Berengaria, who married Richard the Lionheart (King of England from 1189 to 1199), was the daughter of the King of Navarre and never visited England during her husband's lifetime. Richard himself, busy crusading, spent only a few months of his reign in England. *Nick Rennison*

Has New York ever been the capital of the USA?

George Washington's inauguration as the first president of the United States took place in New York in 1789, and the city was the nation's first capital, but only for a year. For the decade 1790–1800 the capital was Philadelphia, but on 11 June 1800 the seat of government was moved to the new city being built on the Potomac River – Washington DC. In 1797 New York City also lost its status as capital of the state of New York. It was replaced by Albany, which has held the honour ever since. *Nick Rennison*

If the Gunpowder Plotters had succeeded in blowing up James I and his parliament, who did they intend should rule the country afterwards?

Their intention was to abduct James's eldest daughter, Princess Elizabeth, then nine years old and staying at Coombe Abbey in Warwickshire, and proclaim her queen. In due course she could be married to a prominent Catholic nobleman, and the country could be returned to Catholicism. A group of men was meant to kidnap Elizabeth from Coombe, but once Guy Fawkes was arrested, the plot rapidly fell apart and the planned abduction of the princess was abandoned. *Nick Rennison*

Did you know...?

Only one delegate signed the American Declaration of Independence on 4 July 1776. John Hancock, president of the Second Continental Congress, put his name to the document on that historic date but most of the other delegates to the Congress actually signed on 2 August of that year. *Nick Rennison*

Did you know...?

The dedication of the Lincoln Memorial in Washington DC in 1922 was segregated. The ceremony to dedicate the most famous monument to the president who freed the slaves was attended by many dignitaries, including Lincoln's only surviving son, but the black guests of honour had to sit in a separate section from the whites. *Nick Rennison*

When Lady Jane Grey was proclaimed queen in 1553 she had a living mother, Frances Brandon, who was a more direct descendant of Henry VII. Why was Jane's mother not considered for the throne?

The answer is, perhaps not surprisingly, political ambition. Lady Jane Grey's claim on the throne was based on the fact that she was a great-granddaughter of Henry VII through her mother Lady Frances Brandon. By both the rules of succession and the Act of Succession passed by Parliament during the reign of Henry VIII, however, she ranked after Henry's two daughters, later queens Mary I and Elizabeth I. However, the Protector of England during the reign of the young King Edward VI was the intensely ambitious John Dudley, Duke of Northumberland. As a Protestant, Northumberland knew that he would be dismissed – and perhaps prosecuted – by the Catholic Mary. He married his son, Lord Guildford Dudley, to Lady Jane in May 1553 when it became clear that Edward was dying. He then persuaded the dying king to name Lady Jane as his successor. This move would make Northumberland's son the consort of the monarch and so give Northumberland far more power and influence than if the new queen had been Jane's mother. In the event, Northumberland's plotting came to nothing. The people of England preferred Mary to Jane. Northumberland was sent to the scaffold a few weeks later, followed by Lady Jane and her husband after an abortive Protestant rebellion convinced Queen Mary that the pair were too dangerous to keep alive. *Rupert Matthews*

10 Statesmen who fought duels

When diplomacy fails a man's just gotta do what a man's gotta do...

1 **Charles James Fox**
Whig politician,
1779

2 **Frederick Duke of York**
British Army commander-in-chief, 1789

3 **William Pitt the Younger**
prime minister,
1798

4 **Aaron Burr**
US vice president,
1804

5 **Alexander Hamilton**
US first secretary of the treasury,
1804 (with Burr)

6 **Andrew Jackson**
future US president,
1806

7 **George Canning**
foreign secretary,
1809

8 **Viscount Castlereagh**
minister of war, 1809
(with Canning)

9 **Duke of Wellington**
prime minister,
1829

10 **Charles Floquet**
French prime minister,
1888

Did the Roman Empire ever consider granting independence or at the very least self-governing status to any of the territories it conquered?

From its very earliest days Rome was a military power famed for annexing neighbouring states, converting allies into provinces and conquering any area when it got the chance. That is not to say, however, that Rome imposed an inflexible oppression on its conquests, nor that it never let them go. A key aim of Rome was to establish an effective local government in the provinces. This would, it was hoped, organise and pay for such things as law and order, local defence, trade regulation and so forth. Of course, this was always under the watchful eye of the local governor, who was ever ready to step in if anything were done that was against Rome's interests.

Granting full independence was another matter entirely. The area of Germany between the Rhine and the Elbe was conquered in a series of campaigns between 12 BC and AD 4. But in AD 9 the three legions in Germany, under the command of Quintilius

Varus, were ambushed in the Teutoburg Forest and all but annihilated. The frontier was pulled back to the Rhine and the German tribes regained their independence. No such military disaster caused the retreat from Armenia, Assyria and Mesopotamia ordered by the Emperor Hadrian in AD 117. Instead, the issue seems to have been cost. The acquisition of the territories greatly enlarged the length of the border that needed to be guarded against the Parthians. Trajan, who conquered the territories, thought the additional cost worthwhile, but his successor, Hadrian, did not. There was no attempt to establish new independent states, or to grant autonomy to local rulers. The Romans simply left and the Parthians moved in.

Similarly, the Romans abandoned most of what is now southern Scotland around AD 163, apparently because the costs of maintaining control far outweighed the benefits. The legions fell back to the older border at Hadrian's Wall. Again, no attempt was made to establish meaningful independence, and the local tribes soon fell under the influence of the Pictish tribes to the north.
Rupert Matthews

Who was the first black Member of Parliament?

The first MPs of Afro-Caribbean descent were returned to parliament in 1987, and they included Diane Abbott, Bernie Grant and Paul Boateng, who was later to become the first black Cabinet minister. However, in July 1892 Dadabhai Naoroji was elected Liberal MP for Finsbury. He was a Parsee, born in Bombay, who had been president of the Indian National Congress and had then moved to England in the 1880s. *Nick Rennison*

When did America first appear as 'America' on a map?

The first-known map to use the term 'America' to designate the landmass of the New World was a world map created by the German cartographer Martin Waldseemüller in 1507. He incorporated geographical information taken from a letter written by the Italian explorer Amerigo Vespucci, and it is usually assumed that he named the new continent after him. A copy of the map is on display at the Library of Congress in Washington.
Nick Rennison

Did you know...?

During the run-up to the Spanish Civil War (1936–9), General Francisco Franco was mockingly known as 'Miss Canary Islands 1936' by the other army officers who were plotting to fight against the republican government. Franco, stationed in the Canary Islands, was seen as girlishly unable to decide whether or not to commit himself to the military coup. *Nick Rennison*

Who was the first ruler of China, and how long did he rule for?

One problem with the earliest Chinese history is that in 206 BC rebels burnt the imperial archives. Scholars acting on orders from the Han emperors later tried to reconstruct the lost archives from partial records stored elsewhere and from the memories of the librarians. The results, as was recognised even then, were incomplete and in places mistaken. According to the reconstructed archives, the 'able and virtuous Yao united the black-haired people and brought harmony to the land' in around 2300 BC. Chinese government was then put on a firmer footing when Yu founded the first imperial dynasty, the Xia, in 2205 BC. But it is now thought that these accounts are at best semi-legendary. In any case, they refer only to the area of the lower Yellow River. The Shang and Zhou dynasties that are recorded as following the Xia are often likewise dismissed as having little or no foundation in fact. However, archaeologists are now turning up evidence that a unified culture – if not a unified state – spread from well north of the Yellow River to the north bank of the Yangtze by around 1100 BC, the time of the late Shang. When Chinese history becomes more reliable, around 600 BC, it reveals that the area occupied by settled farmers and urban cities was divided into independent kingdoms. In 221 BC these were united by Zheng, King of Qin, as the culmination of years of conquest and warfare. Zheng took a new name to emphasise his achievement, calling himself Qin Shi Huangdi, or 'First Qin Sovereign Emperor'. He is the first who can be said with certainty to have ruled over a united Chinese state. It was he who built the great tomb at Mount Li, guarded by the terracotta army of full-size warriors. He died in 210 BC, having ruled all China for 11 years. Although his dynasty was overthrown soon afterwards, the concept of a united China persisted to the present day. *Rupert Matthews*

When did France begin to be called France, rather than by the names of the areas, such as Aquitaine and Normandy?

Some people, the Greeks for instance, never stopped calling the country by its Latin name, Gallia. As late as the 18th century, most of the educated classes of Europe, conversing and corresponding in Latin, called it by the same name the Romans used.

'France' comes from 'Francia', the medieval name, meaning 'the kingdom of the Franks'. The Franks were the Germanic tribe who took over the area after the fall of the Roman Empire, though the modern French state dates from 843 when Charlemagne's vast empire was split into three, with Charles the Bald taking control of the western part. However, Hugh Capet (r. 987–96) was the first to be crowned King of France, though the name referred to the domains of the Capet family in the area around Paris now known as the Ile de France. Hugh's authority over the fiefdoms making up the rest of the country was slim, and it took his successors hundreds of years to create a unified state. Even then, many provincial and feudal privileges lasted down to 1789. The true French republican dates the real foundation of France from the Revolution because until then it was a collection of provinces ruled by aristocrats and kings; only then did it become a nation of people choosing freely to unite.
Eugene Byrne

CHAPTER 9

LAW AND ORDER, OR THE TALE OF THE MAD TRAPPER

Is it true that a Victorian murderer escaped the death penalty because the gallows failed?

In 1885 John Lee was scheduled to be hanged at Exeter for the murder of an elderly spinster. He was positioned on the scaffold three times, but each time the trapdoor failed to open. Lee was taken back to his cell and his sentence commuted to life imprisonment. He was released from Portland Prison in 1907. *Nick Rennison*

In the First World War the British Army executed 351 men for desertion and other offences. Did Germany have a similar policy with their men?

The German Army of 1914–18 was remarkably reluctant to execute its own men. Although it was considerably larger than the British Army, it executed only 48 men. Some German officers remarked on how severe British discipline was. Perhaps the philosophical difference lies in the fact that before the war the German Army was a 'national' force recruited by selective conscription, while the British Army was a regular volunteer force recruited from what was then believed to be the lowest, roughest social classes. The British Army failed to adjust its disciplinary system to take account of the fact that during the war it too became a national force, drawn from every part of society. However, we should never forget that over 90 per cent of British death sentences were commuted. As over 5 million men served in the British Army during the war, the numbers executed were statistically minute, however tragic the individual cases might have been. *Gary Sheffield*

People often used to say – I guess some still do – that we should bring back National Service to reduce youth crime. Is there any evidence that National Service actually kept crime levels low?

Post-war Britain needed conscripts to meet continuing military obligations, so males between the ages of 18 and 26 were expected to serve in the armed forces for 18 months (extended to two years at the time of the Korean War, 1950–3). The last intake of National Servicemen took place in 1960 and the last recruit was discharged in 1963. To many, the end of National Service and the rise of 1960s' youth culture, with its materialism, promiscuity and disrespect, was no coincidence. But with crime rates, the picture is not as simple as fans of National Service believed. Whatever nostalgic ideas we might have, the fact is that crime shot up during the war: rationing and the blackout offered ample opportunities for the criminally minded, while boys were deprived of fathers and other male authority figures and role models because of wartime service. Crime also continued increasing through the 1940s partly because of the easy availability of firearms, as portrayed in the 1950 Ealing drama *The Blue Lamp*, starring Dirk Bogarde as psychotic young tearaway Tom Riley, and Jack Warner as George Dixon, the very ideal of the British bobby.

The early 1950s did see a small fall in crime rates, but overall figures remained much higher than in the 1930s, when there had been no conscription. In 1950 a total of 461,435 offences were recorded in England and Wales; in 1955 it was 438,085; but by 1960 it had risen to 743,713, so there was a huge rise in crime while National Service was still going on. While the youth culture of the 1960s led to moral panic, it's worth remembering that the same thing happened in the 1950s, with lurid newspaper reports of cosh boys, beatniks and teddy boys, who later gave way to mods. National Service might well have done a lot of young men some good, but it did not reduce crime. *Eugene Byrne*

Did you know...?

After his death, the 9th-century pope Formosus was exhumed by his successor, Stephen VI, and his corpse was put on trial for an assortment of crimes he had supposedly committed while alive. *Nick Rennison*

There are endless stories of grave-robbers stealing corpses for the medical profession in the early 19th century, but nothing from mid-Victorian times. Yet surely the doctors needed just as many bodies as ever. When did grave-robbing stop and why?

Under a law of Henry VIII, confirmed by the 1752 Murder Act, the bodies of executed murderers were made available to physicians for study. (The 1752 Act was passed a year after William Hogarth's famous picture *The Reward of Cruelty* depicted a hanged criminal being dissected at Surgeons' Hall.) The expansion of the medical profession in the early 19th century produced a demand for corpses that the criminal justice system could no longer meet. This led to 'resurrectionists' – criminals, and sometimes even doctors and students – robbing fresh graves. Panic really set in when people were murdered to meet the demand for specimens, most notoriously by Edinburgh's William Burke and William Hare, and the copycat London Burkers. The 1832 Anatomy Act largely dealt with the problem. Those wanting to practise anatomy had to obtain a licence, which made them responsible for the proper care of cadavers in their medical institution. The Act allowed 'unclaimed' corpses – usually those who had died in prison or the workhouse – to be taken by anatomists. It also allowed the poor to donate relatives' bodies on condition that they would receive a decent burial after dissection. Individuals were also allowed to leave their own bodies to medical science. The philosopher Jeremy Bentham famously did so, though it would be several decades before many others followed his example. *Eugene Byrne*

When was the last official beheading in England?

The last person to be executed by beheading in England was Simon Fraser, Lord Lovat, on 9 April 1747. Lovat, a wily Scot known as the Old Fox, appears to have been a disreputable character, wheeling and dealing his way through a tumultuous period in British history. He was outlawed twice, once for high treason in 1698, and again in 1701 for abducting and forcibly marrying his brother's widow in an attempt to inherit his estate. After the Battle of Culloden, in which he took no active part but was implicated on the Jacobite side, he fled to an island in Loch Morar, where he was discovered hiding in a hollow tree. He was then taken to London, tried and beheaded on Tower Hill in a public event so popular that a scaffold erected for the benefit of spectators collapsed under their weight, killing 20 people beneath.

Beheading was seen as a more honourable way to die than being hanged, and the punishment was traditionally reserved for criminals of high status: Mary Queen of Scots met her end this way in 1587, as did Sir Walter Raleigh in 1618 and Charles I in 1649. Archbishop Laud, sentenced to death by hanging in 1644, was granted his last wish in 1645 of being beheaded instead. From 1814, hanging became the mode of execution for treason, although the monarch could still order a beheading until it was finally outlawed in 1870. *Steph Gapper*

When was the first identikit picture used to convict a criminal in Britain?

Elsie Batten, an assistant in a shop near London's Charing Cross Road, was stabbed to death in the shop on 3 March 1961. The police created an identikit picture of a man seen acting suspiciously in the vicinity, the first that was ever used by Scotland Yard. On 8 March a police constable saw a man in Old Compton Street who matched the identikit picture and arrested him. Edwin Bush later confessed to killing Mrs Batten. *Nick Rennison*

Is there a rational explanation for the witch-hunts in Salem, Massachusetts, in 1692?

Historians have postulated various explanations for the Salem trials, which saw 185 accusations and the executions of 14 women and five men on charges of witchcraft between February and autumn 1692. Perhaps the best way to understand the trials is to consider the climate of extreme religious fervour that pervaded the settlements of 17th-century Puritan New England. This was particularly prevalent in Salem due to the formidable 'fire and brimstone' minister Samuel Parris, whose daughter Betty and niece Abigail Williams were the first to be 'possessed' and make accusations of witchery. His 'iron fist' household, the repressed situation of women in Puritan society, and Abigail's position as an adopted member of the family have been used as evidence for a medical diagnosis of hysteria to explain their 'affliction'.

As for the pattern of allegations, those accused were generally already regarded as misfits. The ball began rolling with Tituba, the Indian slave in the Parris household, followed by Sarah Good and

Did you know…?

Billy the Kid first came to the law's attention as a 15-year-old, when he was arrested in 1875 for stealing cheese and clothes. A few years later the teenager was the most wanted outlaw in the American West, allegedly responsible for killing a man for each year of his life. *Nick Rennison*

Sarah Osborne, both social outcasts and non-churchgoers. Many of the accused were also people against whom Parris and his allies, the Putnams, had grudges. Once accusations started to spread to more highly regarded citizens, such as the governor's wife, colonial ministers took a stand and the hysteria abated. Finally, tensions within the community, which was split into the prosperous trading area of Salem Town and the disgruntled farming settlement of Salem Village, might further explain the pattern of accusation. The threat of Indian attack, with a frontier war raging not far away, created a society confronted daily with the prospect of violence. Historians conjecture that it was these conditions that fostered the Salem witch-hunts. *Steph Gapper*

Who was the last person to be executed at the Tower of London?

The last person to be executed at the Tower was Josef Jakobs, a German intelligence agent who was parachuted into southern England on 31 January 1941. Injured in landing, he was easily captured and the equipment he was carrying clearly proved that he was a spy. After a swift court-martial, he was executed by firing squad. Because of his injuries, he was shot while sitting down. *Nick Rennison*

Did Sweeney Todd really exist?

Sweeney Todd, the barber who killed his customers and delivered their bodies to Mrs Lovett's Pie Shop to be transformed into meat pies, is one of England's great bogeymen. Despite claims that he was a real person, he was a fictional character and owes his fame to a minor 19th-century playwright, George Dibdin-Pitt, author of a blood-and-thunder melodrama called *The String of Pearls, or The Fiend of Fleet Street*. *Nick Rennison*

10 People who were shot by firing squad

They died for their principles, or because they had none.

1 **Charles Lucas and George Lisle**
English royalists during the Civil War, 1648

2 **John Byng**
British admiral, disobeyed orders, 1757

3 **Duke of Enghien**
French royalist conspirator, 1804

4 **Michel Ney**
Napoleonic marshal, 1815

5 **Maximilian I**
Mexican emperor, shot by republicans, 1867

6 **Edith Cavell**
British nurse and war heroine, shot by Germany, 1915

7 **James Connolly**
Irish nationalist, 1916

8 **Mata Hari**
Dutch dancer and spy, 1917

9 **Claus von Stauffenberg**
German conspirator, 1944

10 **Vidkun Quisling**
Norwegian collaborator, 1945

What was oakum and why did prisoners in the past have to pick it?

Oakum was a type of tarred fibre, which was rammed into the spaces between the planks of a wooden ship to prevent the water getting in. It was made by unpicking and unravelling lengths of rope. The job was painful, monotonous and time-consuming, but it was essential to the navy. Both socially valuable and punishingly unpleasant to do, picking oakum was considered ideal work for prisoners and for those sent to the workhouse. *Nick Rennison*

The medieval Marcher Lords were a famously tough bunch. Which was the toughest?

Charged with maintaining law and order in the notoriously lawless border lands between England and the Welsh principalities, the Marcher Lords maintained private armies and handed out savage justice. They fought each other almost as often as they fought the Welsh. Robert of Rhuddlan, known locally as The Terror, has a good claim to be the most ruthless. He built a castle at Rhuddlan in

1073 on the site of what had been the royal seat of Gruffydd ap Llywelyn, King of Gwynedd. Robert had been given all of North Wales by William the Conqueror, although the king had no right to do so. Robert found his new estates firmly in the hands of the local Welsh lords, so he embarked on a career of bloodshed, deceit and violence that, partially at least, won him the lands he coveted.

Less successful in the long run was Roger Mortimer, Earl of March. In 1322 he was imprisoned in the Tower of London for treason. Mortimer escaped – no mean feat – in 1323 and fled to France. There he met King Edward II's estranged queen and seduced her. In 1326 the pair returned to England and raised a rebellion. Edward II was ousted from his throne and murdered in brutal fashion. The young Edward III was installed as a puppet king by Mortimer, who executed his personal enemies and grabbed vast estates by rigging legal cases. Imposing his rule with foreign mercenaries, Mortimer seemed unassailable, until caught one night in a plot involving young Edward III. Mortimer was dragged to Tyburn and hanged as a common criminal.
Rupert Matthews

Was Britain ever tempted to copy the USA in the 1920s and bring in prohibition of the sale of alcohol?

Prohibition in the USA was the culmination of nearly 100 years of campaigning. As Americans in the 19th century worked to get liquor banned or restricted in individual states, British temperance campaigners called for a different strategy – a law enabling local authorities to withdraw pub licences if ratepayers voted for it. The First World War gave the temperance lobby much of what it wanted. David Lloyd George (who famously said that Britain had 'three enemies – Germany, Austria and drink') oversaw a draconian code of laws that restricted pub opening hours, reduced beer strength and even forbade the buying of rounds. In Bristol a man was prosecuted for buying his own wife a drink.

Beer remained weak and licensing hours strict until the 1980s, which reduced beer consumption and arrests for drunkenness. This pacified many would-be prohibitionists, and deterred them from what they saw as American hypocrisy – a society that banned drink, yet consumed vast quantities of bootleg booze, creating a crime wave in the process. *Eugene Byrne*

My brother in Australia swears blind that Australian banknotes used to feature the portrait of a man who was a convicted forger. Can this be true?

Yes, indeed, although – sadly – the convict in question was not a forger of banknotes. His name was Francis Greenway (1777–1837), and he was born at Mangotsfield, near Bristol. The son of a mason, he trained under the architect John Nash before setting up a building business in Bristol with his two brothers. This firm went bankrupt in 1809, and Greenway was later accused of forging a building contract in connection with this failure. He pleaded guilty in 1812 and was sentenced to transportation to Australia for life. When he arrived in 1814 the New South Wales colony was still in its infancy. His building skills were soon in demand, and Governor Lachlan Macquarie became an enthusiastic patron. By 1816 he was acting civil architect of New South Wales. He was conditionally emancipated (freed) the following year, and his wife Mary and their children went out to join him. During this time he was responsible for several buildings, including the Macquarie Lighthouse, three churches, the stables at Government House, Fort Macquarie at Benelong Point, and the Hyde Park convict barracks. The last of these commissions earned him a full pardon.

In person Greenway was said to be arrogant and bad-tempered, and after Macquarie's departure he got no further large commissions. He carried on in private practice without much success until retiring to his convict land-grant property on the Hunter River, where he died. There are around 50 buildings still standing in Sydney that are attributed to Greenway, most of them dating from his period of frantic activity under Macquarie. Although the cynical might point out that he didn't have much competition, architectural historians find a lot to admire in his work, and he can reasonably claim to be the father of Australian architecture. The country honoured him by featuring his portrait on the $10 note from 1966 to 1993. *Eugene Byrne*

Why are the Home Counties so named?

The Home Counties is a term loosely used to mean the southeast of England, but excluding London. More strictly, it refers to those counties that border the Greater London area: Surrey, Kent, Essex, Hertfordshire, Buckinghamshire and (since 1995) Berkshire. The phrase originated in the medieval criminal court

Did you know...?

The organisation that became the FBI was founded by a member of Napoleon's family. Charles-Joseph Bonaparte, grandson of Napoleon's youngest brother, was born in Baltimore and created the Bureau of Investigation, later the Federal Bureau of Investigation, in 1908 when he was serving as attorney-general in President Theodore Roosevelt's Cabinet. *Nick Rennison*

system known as the Assizes. This system, which takes its name from the French *assises*, dates back to regulations drawn up in 1166, but they were subject to various changes and alterations until abolished in 1971. The Assizes became the most senior of the usual criminal courts, trying those cases deemed too serious or complex to be dealt with by the Justices of the Peace or local county courts. They were presided over by senior judges from the King's (or Queen's) Bench in Westminster. These judges went out on tours of the country to try such cases as demanded by the amount of business – usually once or twice each year.

By around 1300 these periodic tours had begun to follow a number of set itineraries, known as circuits. The judge and his entourage stopped at the larger towns to hear cases from the locality. The Assize Circuit that covered the area around London was termed the Home Circuit, as it was closest to the homes of the judges involved. Reforms in the 19th century transferred much of the business of the Home Circuit to the Central Criminal Court – otherwise known as the Old Bailey – and the remainder was transferred to Crown Courts in 1971. By then, however, the name 'Home Counties' had stuck and still does. *Rupert Matthews*

Why were fraudulent doctors and medical practitioners known as 'quacks'?

The word 'quack', meaning an untrained person pretending to be a doctor, is an abbreviation of 'quacksalver'. In early modern Dutch *kwakzalver* meant a person who boasted of the miraculous properties of his medicines. Some time in the 16th century (the first reference in *The Oxford English Dictionary* dates from the 1590s), the word crossed over into the English language and was later shortened and used to refer to medical charlatans of all kinds. *Nick Rennison*

Do you have any information on a man known as Albert Johnson or 'The Mad Trapper'?

On 9 July 1931 a stranger arrived on the Mackenzie Delta of Canada's Northwest Territories, giving his name as Albert Johnson. By December trappers were complaining that someone was stealing animals from their traps. On 31 December the Mounties, Canada's Mounted Police, arrived at Johnson's cabin to ask him some questions, then returned with warrants two days later. Johnson replied with a fusillade of rifle bullets, which badly wounded a Constable King. The Mounties then sent out several patrols and, on 30 January 1932, one of them located the man who had become known across Canada as 'The Mad Trapper'. One Mountie was shot dead and Johnson escaped again. Over 200 men, including Inuit trackers, were now chasing the fugitive. Radio reporters were giving live reports of their progress, and all of Canada was transfixed by the affair.

A Mountie patrol finally caught up with the Mad Trapper on 17 February, having been given the position of his camp by a spotter aircraft – the first used in a manhunt. Johnson was killed in the resulting gun battle, though it took nine bullets to bring him down. The body was found to have a small fortune on it, but no identity documents. It transpired that Albert Johnson was a false name, and the dead man's fingerprints were not recorded in Canada, the USA or Britain. Where the Mad Trapper had come from, why he opened fire and how he managed to survive the Canadian wilderness in midwinter for five weeks remain complete mysteries.
Rupert Matthews

There is a song called 'The Man Who Broke the Bank at Monte Carlo'. Who was the man and did he really break the bank?

In 1873 Joseph Jaggers, a Yorkshire engineer, devised a system to beat the bank in a Monte Carlo casino. Jaggers won more than $300,000 (millions in today's money) before the casino found a way to stop him. The song that celebrates his achievements was published in 1892, the year he died. *Nick Rennison*

10 Inmates of Bedlam

Now in Beckenham, Kent, the Bethlem Royal Hospital, or 'Bedlam', is one of the world's oldest mental hospitals. Its Southwark buildings now house the Imperial War Museum.

1 **Mary Frith,**
   aka Moll Cutpurse
   (died 1659) thief

2 **Nathaniel Lee**
   (1653–92)
   dramatist

3 **Hannah Snell**
   (1723–92)
   female soldier

4 **Jonathan Martin**
   (died 1838) brother
   of painter John Martin;
   set fire to York
   Minster

5 **Augustus Pugin**
   (1812–52) architect

6 **Richard Dadd**
   (1817–86) artist;
   murdered his father

7 **Edward Oxford**
   (born 1822) tried to shoot
   Queen Victoria and Prince
   Albert

8 **George Gilbert Scott**
   (1839–97) architect; surveyor
   of Westminster Abbey

9 **Louis Wain**
   (1860–1939)
   'The man who drew cats'

10 **Eirene Botting,**
   aka Antonia White
   (1899–1980) novelist

What are the origins of the Ku Klux Klan?

After the American Civil War of 1861–5, the economy of the defeated southern or Confederate states was disrupted and many farms laid to waste, so poverty and starvation stalked the land. The victorious Union enforced martial law and allowed northern businessmen, known as 'carpetbaggers', to exploit the situation by buying up farms and factories at bargain prices. The Union troops were too few – and often had no inclination – to halt the widespread banditry and lawlessness of the time. On 24 December 1865, at Pulaski, Tennessee, a group of former Confederate army officers decided to form a secret club that would enforce some kind of order on the neighbourhood and give the local whites a sense of hope and solidarity. Led by Captain John Lester the men took the word 'klux' from the Greek for 'circle', chose 'klan' as they were all of Scottish or Irish descent, and finally added 'ku' simply because it sounded good. The men adopted false names and dressed in white cloaks and hoods to hide their identities. They put about the story that the strange white-robed figures that rode at night were the ghosts of Confederate soldiers come to avenge themselves on the wicked.

The KKK, as the Klan became known, spread rapidly across the southern states. Some joined to crack down on lawlessness, some to oppose rule by the Union military, and others out of racist motives to persecute former slaves. Some members indulged in brutal violence, but others put their efforts into peaceful protest and political work. By 1872 the southern states had regained some measure of self-rule, while law and order had been re-established. The KKK movement quickly collapsed. In 1915 director D.W. Griffith made the film *Birth of a Nation*, which showed the Klan in a positive, even glamorous light. This inspired retired officer 'Colonel' William Simmons to found the New Klan in Georgia as what he called 'a patriotic, Christian organisation' open to white men only. At one time the New Klan had 5 million members, but a series of financial scandals caused its decline, and during the Second World War it ceased to exist as a national organisation. Some local chapters survived and formed the base for the modern KKK movement.
Rupert Matthews

Did you know…?

In 1882, would-be poet Roderick MacLean shot a pistol at Queen Victoria at Windsor Station. He missed. MacLean attempted the assassination because he had mailed one of his poems to the queen and she had not sent him a sufficiently favourable response.
Nick Rennison

A brief article about my great-great-grandmother's funeral in a local newspaper from 1898 says that the ceremony was 'attended by many prominent members of the Bristol and South Western Counties branch of the National Vigilance Association'. What was this sinister-sounding organisation?

The National Vigilance Association (NVA), formed in August 1885, brought together a number of different strands of Victorian social concern. While it remains intensely interesting to feminist historians, it's been almost completely lost from mainstream memory, which is odd considering how influential it was. The immediate catalyst for the NVA was a series of sensational articles about child prostitution by the muckraking journalist W.T. Stead. They were influential in persuading politicians to pass the 1885 Criminal Law Amendment Act, which raised the age of consent from 13 to 16 and laid out penalties for sexual offences against women and children. The NVA was formed 'for the enforcement and improvement of the laws for the repression of criminal vice and public immorality', and its founders included Stead himself, as well as the social reformers Josephine Butler and Millicent Fawcett. Much of the impetus came from a widespread realisation that the State alone could not be relied on to enforce the Act, and that 'vigilance' by the public would be needed.

The NVA quickly absorbed and/or amalgamated with several other organisations campaigning for public morality (including the venerable Society for the Suppression of Vice, whose £50 bank balance the NVA inherited), and for the rights of women and children. It brought thousands of women into active public life, so was a vital forerunner of the suffragette movement. It was soon also pressing for the censorship of pornography and corrupting art. One of its earliest campaigns, for example, was to prevent some of Emile Zola's novels being published in Britain. Much of its lobbying can appear ridiculously puritanical, but at heart the NVA was a progressive organisation. It did much good work to publicise and suppress people-trafficking and sexual exploitation of women and children well into the 20th century, not just in Britain, but within the empire and overseas as well.
Eugene Byrne

Were there ever any opium dens in Britain, or was this just a scare story put about by xenophobic Victorians?

The Chinese diasporas of the 19th and 20th centuries brought Chinese communities to cities, especially ports, throughout the world, and opium addicts took their habits with them. Opium 'dens' tended to be frequented by more transient and mobile addicts, such as sailors and casual labourers. The richly furnished, opulent dens of Western imagination were comparatively rare; the typical den in, say, San Francisco's Chinatown was usually pretty squalid. It has become fashionable lately, however, to question whether they existed at all in Britain. They may be a racist myth, the product of Western neuroses about the 'Yellow Peril' and white slavery, plus fictional mentions in stories by

10 People whose heads were displayed on London Bridge

Decapitation didn't prevent these doomed notables from showing their faces on the streets of London.

1 **William Wallace**
Scottish patriot, 1305

2 **Hugh Despenser the Younger**
royal favourite, 1326

3 **Simon of Sudbury**
Archbishop of Canterbury, 1381

4 **Henry Percy**
1st Earl of Northumberland, magnate and rebel, 1408

5 **Jack Cade**
leader of the Kent Rebellion, 1450

6 **Elizabeth Barton**
the 'Holy Maid of Kent', visionary, 1534

7 **Thomas More**
statesman and martyr, 1535

8 **Thomas Cromwell**
royal minister, 1540

9 **Robert Catesby**
gunpowder plotter, 1605

10 **Hugh Peter**
Cromwellian minister, 1660

Arthur Conan Doyle, Oscar Wilde, Charles Dickens, Agatha Christie and others.

The case against British opium dens rests partly on the fact that nobody has yet come up with a photograph of one, and the rather more logical point that opium and laudanum were freely and openly available without prescription from pharmacies, so why would anyone need illicit premises and suppliers? But you wouldn't expect the photographic record to be that extensive, and transitory Chinese people with little knowledge of the local language and customs would surely prefer the company of their compatriots. A quick search of 19th-century provincial newspapers turns up numerous reports of deaths and other incidents at Chinese-owned properties in Britain where opium was consumed. Even *The Times* archive turns up Chinese people being arrested for supplying opium at premises in Glasgow, Liverpool and, of course, London's Limehouse. There is a spike in reports of arrests and court cases relating to opium during and after the First World War, presumably because of the presence of larger than usual numbers of Chinese labourers and sailors brought in for war work, and also because the Defence of the Realm Acts of 1914 and 1915 were as severe on drugs (particularly opium and cocaine) as they were – notoriously – on pub opening hours. *Eugene Byrne*

I remember my mother once telling me a story about a gentleman-criminal who was sentenced to death in Victorian times, but who escaped death by inserting a silver tube into his windpipe, thus preventing strangulation by the hangman's noose. True or not?

As an urban legend, the use of a silver tube to cheat the noose probably originated in the use of such 'implants' by 18th/19th-century doctors to aid patients with injuries or illnesses that made it difficult to breathe or swallow freely. There are at least two cases in which felons were said to have tried it. Henry Fauntleroy (1784–1824), a respectable banker, overspent on his extravagant lifestyle and expensive mistresses, and ended up embezzling around £250,000 of his clients' money. His execution outside Newgate Prison drew a crowd of 100,000. Afterwards it was claimed that he had had a silver tube, and that his friends had carried him off while he was still alive.

There is no evidence whatever for this; someone was placed in the family vault at Bunhill Fields after the hanging, and the body delivered was almost certainly that of Henry Fauntleroy.

The most famous case concerns Deacon William Brodie (1741–88), a respectable Edinburgh cabinet-maker, councillor and churchman by day, and a thief and burglar by night. His nocturnal escapades were partly to fund his gambling and womanising, but partly also because he just liked the thrill of it. The author Robert Louis Stevenson, whose father owned some furniture made by Brodie, was later inspired by this tale of a double life to write *The Strange Case of Dr Jekyll and Mr Hyde* (1886). When Brodie eventually went to the gallows – which he had helped to design some years previously! – he was said to be wearing a steel collar (that he allegedly bribed the hangman to ignore), and had a silver tube down his throat as well. Contemporary eyewitness accounts, however, say his neck was clearly bare. After he was hanged his friends took him to an apothecary and tried to revive him, but without success. The story later spread that he had escaped to Paris.
Eugene Byrne

CHAPTER 10

INVENTION AND EXPLORATION, OR THE SEA URCHIN THAT WENT INTO SPACE

Who invented roller-skates?

In 1760 the Belgian Joseph Merlin, a London instrument-maker and inventor, showed off the world's first roller-skates when he glided through a London society ball, wearing metal-wheeled boots and playing a violin. Unfortunately, Merlin had omitted to equip his skates with any braking mechanism, and he crashed into a mirror, injuring himself severely. *Nick Rennison*

When were illuminated adverts first put up in Piccadilly Circus, and what did they advertise?

Photographs show that electrical adverts first appeared in Piccadilly around the turn of the 20th century. Mellin's Pharmacy, which was situated where Regent Street entered the Circus, had a large illuminated sign advertising itself in 1904. The first such adverts for major companies that are still in business today were erected by Perrier in 1908 and Bovril and Schweppes in 1910. Strictly speaking, the signs were against planning law, but they rapidly became tourist attractions. Within a few years, Piccadilly Circus was ablaze with these lights and it has remained so. *Nick Rennison*

Why is the state of New South Wales in Australia so called? It looks nothing like South Wales.

Captain Cook sailed up the east coast of Australia (then known as New Holland) between April and August 1770, naming various places along the way, including Botany Bay. The first reference he makes to naming the region is not until 22 August 1770, when he reached Torres Strait, claiming 'the whole Eastern Coast from the above Latitude [38 degrees South] down to this place by the Name of New South Wales' for the Crown. He gave no reasons for his choice, so most people assume he thought it did look like South Wales – bear in mind that he didn't go very far inland.

However, it might just have been the next step in the colonial trend of naming far-flung parts of the world after places back home. There was already a New England (in America) and a Nova Scotia (in Canada), so 'New Wales' would have been the next logical choice. His journal entry looks as though this is what he originally went for, before finding out that there already was one (in what is now northwestern Canada) and inserting a 'South'. Ironically, the place whose name he was trying not to duplicate was already called New South Wales. *Steph Gapper*

When and what was the first plastic surgery operation?

The earliest plastic surgery operation to be recorded was carried out on 23 October 1814 at York Hospital, Chelsea, by Joseph Carpue. The procedure aimed to rebuild the nose of an unnamed army officer who had lost most of his soft nasal tissue because of an accidental case of mercury poisoning.

Carpue first drew an inverted outline of the nose on the forehead. He then cut through the skin and pulled the resulting flap down and over to cover the officer's nasal bones. The graft took successfully, while the forehead regrew a patch of skin to replace the piece that had been used in the surgery. The result was rather unsightly and resembled scar tissue as much as skin, but was judged a success. However, Carpue claimed that he had merely adapted a procedure used on a bullock driver in the British Army in India, who lost part of his nose in an accident. The date and precise nature of this earlier operation are unknown. *Rupert Matthews*

When did explorers abandon the term 'Ocean Sea', as used by Christopher Columbus, and replace it with the older 'Atlantic Ocean'?

The term 'Ocean Sea' is much older than Columbus. In the days of ancient Greece it was thought that Europe, Asia and Africa were the only continents. These were surrounded by a vast body of water, called Ocean, in which lay a few islands, such as Britain. This idea persisted throughout medieval times in Europe and in Muslim countries, as both drew their ideas of geography from the classical world. When lobbying to get money and ships from the rulers of Europe, Columbus claimed to be able to cross the 'Ocean Sea' from east to west. This would take him from Europe to Asia. As we now know, he found the Americas. Within 50 years of the voyage of Columbus, cartographers were naming that part of the Ocean that lay between Europe and America 'Atlantic Ocean', while the part that lay between the Americas and China was the 'Pacific Ocean'. Later the term 'Indian Ocean' was coined for the part of the Ocean that lay south of Asia. By around 1580 the idea of one all-encompassing Ocean had been discarded, as explorers discovered the true nature of the layout of the world's landmasses. *Rupert Matthews*

Who invented the aerosol can?

The first recognisably modern aerosol can was patented in 1927 by a Norwegian, Erik Rotheim, who was looking for an efficient way of applying wax to his skis, and discovered that a pressurised spray can delivered the best results. However, the commercial possibilities of aerosols were only realised after the Second World War and US government-sponsored research into a portable means by which soldiers could spray insecticides on malaria-carrying mosquitoes. *Nick Rennison*

Did you know...?

The earliest eyewitness reports of the Wright Brothers' first aeroplane flight appeared in a beekeeping magazine. Amos Root, a beekeeper and businessman, was on hand to see several early flights in Ohio. He offered an article about them to *Scientific American*, but the editor turned it down, so Root published it in a journal about his hobby. *Nick Rennison*

The Soviets sent dogs into space and the Americans sent monkeys, but have other animals ever been space travellers?

During the space race, scientists and researchers from several nations sent an entire menagerie into orbit. Two mice called Laska and Benjy were dispatched by the Americans in 1958, the French launched a cat named Félicette, and the Russians placed guinea pigs, frogs and even a tortoise in their rockets in the late 1960s. In more recent decades, experiments on the space shuttles have involved a wide range of living creatures, from newts and snails to sea urchins, silkworms and spiders. *Nick Rennison*

Why was it that advanced civilisations, such as the Mayas and the Aztecs, never journeyed across the seas and discovered Europe, for example?

As far as most pre-industrial societies were concerned, the seas were dangerous and alien places where there was no good reason to venture, except for fishing close to the shore. Comparatively few peoples before medieval times have been seaborne explorers and colonists; the most significant exception was probably the Austronesians, who spread across the Pacific and Indian Oceans between roughly 2000 BC and AD 500. So rather than ask why the Mayas or Aztecs didn't discover Europe, it's better to ask why Europeans discovered America.

The geography of the Mediterranean and northwest Europe lent itself particularly well to seaborne trade and transport, and from the Phoenicians through to the Vikings and later, the Continent developed high levels of proficiency in shipbuilding and navigation. By the 15th century, Europe comprised a large number of small states in close proximity locked into competition with one another, so exploration and overseas empires brought advantages that prompted rivals to try to catch up. But it is important to remember that by the 15th century, a few other societies, such as China, Japan and some Arab and North African states, were equally sophisticated seafarers, who, in different circumstances, might also have claimed the Americas. Imagine how differently world history might have developed if one of the enormous expeditionary fleets led by the Chinese admiral Zheng He in the early 15th century had crossed the Pacific.
Eugene Byrne

When was the first escalator installed on the London Underground?

The first escalator on the Tube was introduced at Earl's Court Station in 1911. Many people were wary of using the new-fangled apparatus, so 'Bumper' Harris, a man with a wooden leg, was employed to ride on it throughout the day in order to demonstrate how safe it was. The gimmick nearly backfired when some passengers began to speculate on how Harris had originally lost his leg, but soon other, more daring travellers were making detours to Earl's Court to ride the escalator. *Nick Rennison*

When was the first use of electricity?

It depends what you mean by 'use'. The ancient Greeks knew that if you rubbed a stick of *elektron* (amber) with a cloth, you could produce an attractive force that would pick up feathers, but this is hardly 'useful'. Electric currents were used by experimenters such as Humphry Davy in the early 19th century to make all sorts of discoveries about the nature of chemical elements. In practical terms, though, the first major use of electricity was to send long-range messages via telegraph.

The mechanism for communicating using electricity was devised by British entrepreneurs Charles Wheatstone and William Fothergill Cooke, and demonstrated in 1837. It came into operation in Britain in 1839 with a telegraph line running between Paddington and West Drayton, commissioned by the Great Western Railway. Electricity passed down the cables caused needles at the other end to move and point to letters on a dial. It was time-consuming and inaccurate, and eventually the company pulled their funding and Cooke had to pay for the expense of running the wire out of his own pocket.

On the other side of the Atlantic, Alfred Vail and Samuel Morse had been working independently on a similar electrical system, using a series of dots and dashes, that would revolutionise long-range communication. On 24 May 1844 they sent the first official message along the new telegraph line between Washington and Baltimore: 'What hath God wrought.' In 1845 the first public telegraphs came into operation in the USA and Britain.
Steph Gapper

Were bloomers really invented by a woman named Mrs Bloomer?

Amelia Bloomer was a 19th-century American feminist who edited a weekly magazine called *The Lily*. She advocated more sensible and less restrictive clothing for women, and the new outfits she championed included the ankle-length undergarments that were eventually named after her. However, the designer of the first 'bloomers' was actually another American feminist named Elizabeth Smith Miller. Clearly, 'bloomers' was a more memorable name than 'millers'. *Nick Rennison*

Wish I hadn't said that...

'Space travel is utter bilge.'

Astronomer Royal Sir Richard Woolley, 1956. Five years later Yuri Gagarin became the first man in space.

Who invented sunglasses?

Coloured glass may have been used for centuries as a means of protecting the eyes, but James Ayscough, a maker of optical and scientific instruments in mid-18th-century London, was probably the first man to experiment seriously with tinted lenses in spectacles. His glasses were intended to correct problems of vision rather than to shield the eyes from the sun, but they were, in effect, the world's first sunglasses.
Nick Rennison

In the book *1421* by Gavin Menzies, the author claims that voyages from China reached Australia, North America and many other places supposedly discovered many years later by Europeans. Is there academic support for these theories?

During the early 15th century, Chinese emperors ordered a series of remarkable voyages into the Indian Ocean and beyond. They were headed by the court eunuch Zheng He, and the accepted view is that they reached the east coast of Africa and no further. However, in his 2002 bestseller *1421: The Year China Discovered the World*, retired submarine commander Gavin Menzies posited that during the sixth voyage, elements of Zheng's fleets also journeyed to North and South America, Australia, New Zealand, Greenland and Antarctica, setting up colonies as they went. It was an audacious theory that, if proven, could have rewritten the history of global exploration.

The book became a publishing sensation, but the reaction from academics was far more muted. In a review for the *BBC History Magazine*, Dr Jerry Brotton wrote that Menzies 'fails to completely convince that Chinese contact [with the

New World] definitely dates from the 1420s'. Others were less polite, including historian Felipe Fernández-Armesto, who described *1421* as 'heroically defiant of logic, evidence, scholarship and sense'. An international group of scholars has set up a website dedicated to debunking Menzies' theories at www.1421exposed.com. For many academics, Menzies' assertions were so extraordinary that they needed to be supported by a great deal of evidence. This, they felt, was not forthcoming. In his biography of Zheng He, Chinese scholar Edward L. Dreyer complained, 'there is no evidence for any of this [Menzies' claims] in the Chinese sources'. Even when evidence was produced by the author, many felt it had not been analysed with sufficient rigour. An oft-quoted example is an inscription that Menzies discovered in the Cape Verde Islands, which he believed was written in an Indian language. Rather than submit it to an academic authority, he faxed it to the Bank of India for an explanation. While academics have largely challenged *1421*, the book does have many supporters around the globe, and Menzies himself remains defiant. See www.1421.tv for arguments in favour of his hypothesis. *Rob Attar*

When were traffic lights first installed in Britain?

The first traffic lights were installed in Westminster in 1868. They consisted of a revolving lantern with red and green signals. Only months after installation, the gas-powered lights exploded and seriously hurt the policeman operating them.
Nick Rennison

Why do Victorians all look so solemn in photographs? Didn't they know how to say 'cheese'?

It's safe to assume that Victorians smiled as often as we do, but their smiles could rarely be caught on camera. Exposure times for early cameras were so long (several minutes at least) that it was almost impossible for the sitter to keep smiling long enough. Hence the rather fixed and serious expression on the face of nearly everyone in Victorian photographs. *Nick Rennison*

Who invented windscreen wipers for cars?

The first patent for windscreen wipers was issued to a woman from Birmingham, Alabama, in 1903. Reportedly, Mary Anderson noticed on a visit to New York that when it snowed the drivers of trolley-cars either had to leave the front windows open and expose themselves and passengers to the weather, or get out every few minutes to wipe their windscreen by hand. Anderson came up with a device that could be operated by hand from inside the car. Sadly, she made little money from her invention since no manufacturer could see the value of it.
Nick Rennison

A friend told me recently that an Englishman walked across America in the 16th century. Can this really be true?

It depends what you mean by 'across America'. Your friend probably heard the story of David Ingram. In 1568 he was one of a hundred men cast away on the Gulf of Mexico by John Hawkins. Eleven months later, Ingram and two others approached French traders in what is now Nova Scotia. They had walked thousands of miles through present-day Mexico, USA and Canada. Ingram's astonishing story was told in the first edition of English writer Richard Hakluyt's *The Principal Navigations, Voyages, Traffiques and Discoveries of the English Nation* published in 1589. *Nick Rennison*

Everyone knows that Neil Armstrong was the first person to land on the moon, but who was the last person to do so?

The last of 12 American astronauts to walk on the moon was Chicago-born Eugene Cernan in December 1972. Cernan was commander of *Apollo 17*, the final mission to land men on the moon, and he took part in three of what NASA called 'extra-vehicular activities' on its surface. As the commander, he was the last to climb back into the lunar module. While doing so, he said: 'We leave as we came, and, God willing, we shall return, with peace and hope for all mankind.' As yet, we still haven't done so.
Nick Rennison

10 Talents from overseas

Although they were born abroad, these artists found fame (and in some cases fortune) working in Britain.

1 **Hans Holbein**
   (1497–1543) born Augsburg, Germany

2 **Sir Peter Paul Rubens**
   (1577–1640) born Siegen, Westphalia, Germany

3 **Sir Anthony Van Dyck**
   (1599–1641) born Antwerp, Netherlands

4 **Sir Peter Lely**
   (1618–80) born Soest, Westphalia, Germany

5 **Sir Godfrey Kneller**
   (1646–1723) born Lübeck, Germany

6 **Louis Laguerre**
   (1663–1721) born Versailles, France

7 **John Singleton Copley**
   (1738–1815) born Boston, Massachusetts, USA

8 **Camille Pissarro**
   (1830–1903) born St Thomas, West Indies

9 **James McNeill Whistler**
   (1834–1903) born Lowell, Massachusetts, USA

10 **Sir Lawrence Alma-Tadema**
   (1836–1912) born Dronrjip, Netherlands

In the very first telephone message, Alexander Graham Bell said to his assistant in another room, 'Mr Watson, come here. I want to see you.' Was the very first email message similarly banal?

The first email message sent between two computers was so banal that the man who sent it cannot remember for certain what it was. Computer engineer Ray Tomlinson worked on a system for sending mail from machine to machine in 1971, and the first messages were test ones. According to Tomlinson, 'the test messages were entirely forgettable and I have therefore forgotten them'. He thinks it most likely that the first message was 'QWERTYUIOP (the top row of letters on a keyboard) or something similar'. *Nick Rennison*

We know that some members of Ferdinand Magellan's crew were the first men to circumnavigate the world, but do we know who was the first woman to do so?

The first woman to circumnavigate the world spent part of the journey disguised as a man. Jeanne Baret (sometimes spelt Baré) was the mistress of Philibert de Commerson, a naturalist on an expedition led by French navigator Louis Antoine de Bougainville in 1766–9. She took ship disguised as his male valet, and was apparently convincing enough to fool de Bougainville, but was immediately rumbled by the natives when the expedition arrived in Tahiti. Baret completed the circumnavigation as a woman, but was barred from continuing to share a cabin with de Commerson.
Nick Rennison

CHAPTER 11

WAR,
OR
THE SECRET OF
GENGHIS KHAN'S
UNDERWEAR

Is it true that a crossword compiler was arrested just before D-Day on suspicion of sending messages to the Nazis via his crosswords?

It is true. In the weeks before the highly secret D-Day landings on 6 June 1944, those in the know were appalled to discover that clues in the *Daily Telegraph* crosswords led to the answers 'Juno', 'Utah', 'Omaha', 'Mulberry' and 'Overlord' – all key codewords in the planning of the invasion of Normandy. The compiler, schoolmaster Leonard Dawe, was arrested and questioned, and finally convinced the authorities that it was a coincidence. One of Dawe's pupils confessed in the 1980s that he had learnt of the codewords from Canadian soldiers stationed nearby, and suggested them as answers when asked to help with Dawe's crosswords. *Nick Rennison*

Is it true that the *Titanic* had a sister ship that also sank?

The *Titanic* was one of three sister ships owned by the White Star line, the others being the *Olympic* and the *Britannic*. Although the *Olympic* survived until 1935, the *Britannic* sank in the Mediterranean during the First World War, where it was serving as a hospital ship. Most likely the victim of mines laid by a U-boat, the ship was sailing to a Greek island when an explosion sent her to the bottom of the sea. Thirty of the crew and passengers died. *Nick Rennison*

If the Americans hadn't joined the Second World War, would I be speaking German now?

Without American (and Soviet) support, Britain was highly unlikely to have ended up on the winning side. That does not mean that Britain would have been defeated, as an invasion of the UK was nearly impossible in the face of British naval supremacy. Without American intervention, and assuming that the Russo-German War followed roughly the same course, it is likely that the clash between Britain and Germany would have been a stalemate. The Russians were the principal contributors to Hitler's defeat by tying down and destroying the bulk of German troops in the East. If the USSR had been defeated and the USA had remained neutral, perhaps Britain would have been forced to make peace. Even if Britain was not occupied, the best it could have hoped for was the status of a vassal state in the Nazi empire. This is not to underplay the significance of American finance, industrial resources and aid to the British war effort. Moreover, the Americans and Canadians played a critical role in what was arguably the single most significant campaign for Britain – the Battle of the Atlantic. By mid-1943 a massive Allied effort thwarted Hitler's attempt to starve Britain into submission by sinking merchant ships. Without the USA, the prospects for Britain in the war would have been grim indeed. *Gary Sheffield*

I was evacuated to Pen-y-Cae, near Wrexham, in 1939. During language lessons we often read a German newspaper, *Die Zeitung*, which was published in this country. What is the history of this newspaper?

Die Zeitung is German for 'the newspaper', but it is a fair bet that you're referring to *Die Zeitung – Londoner Deutsches Wochenblatt*, which was published in London from 1941 to 1945. The paper was the idea of Sebastian Haffner (real name Raimund Pretzel, 1907–99), a non-Jewish German journalist who had fled the Nazi regime in 1938. It was written by and for German exiles, and was initially four pages, published daily (except Sundays), and costing a penny. In 1942, though, it went weekly, having 12 pages and costing 3d.

The publication was supervised by the government. Although its primary market was German exiles living in Britain, smaller editions were dropped over Germany in leaflet form and distributed to German speakers elsewhere in the world, particularly South

Did you know...?

Genghis Khan's much-feared Mongol warriors wore Chinese silk underwear whenever possible when they rode into battle. Silk is a tough substance and acted as both an extra layer of armour and as a means of drawing out those arrows that did penetrate it.
Nick Rennison

America. Most of its content was news and world affairs, provided by Reuters and Associated Press. It also had a women's section. Haffner's aim was for the paper to stop German exiles thinking of themselves as refugees, and to consider themselves instead as fighters for a free Germany. 'Responsibility for the German future lies with German exiles, and not in Germany,' Haffner said. Unfortunately, he fell out with many of his left-wing colleagues, who regarded him as politically naive, and who mistrusted him for staying in Germany for five years after the Nazis had come to power. Haffner eventually left the paper and joined the *Observer*. His memoir of the rise of the Nazis, *Defying Hitler*, was published after his death and is still available. *Eugene Byrne*

Why was cavalry effective in Palestine, but not on the Western Front in the First World War?

This question is more complicated than it initially appears. During the First World War, while there were mounted charges, cavalry also acted as mounted infantry – using their horses for mobility, but then dismounting and fighting as infantry. In the open warfare at the beginning and end of the war in France in 1914 and 1918, cavalry was quite effective, and even under conditions of trench warfare, there were occasions in which cavalry did well, such as in 1916 at High Wood. The idea that cavalry was completely useless on the Western Front is quite wrong. The trenches in Palestine had less barbed wire and smaller armies than on the Western Front. This meant that defences were more porous than in France and Belgium, offering greater scope for mounted action. General Allenby's campaign in Palestine in 1918 was remarkably modern, coordinating infantry, artillery, cavalry and aeroplanes in a battle resembling the Blitzkrieg of the Second World War – but with horses. *Gary Sheffield*

Is there any truth in the stories that German U-boats refuelled in Ireland during the Second World War?

Although tens of thousands of Irish people served in the British forces and worked in British industries (while almost none went to Germany), Eire maintained a façade of strict neutrality throughout the war. Politically, Irish prime minister Eamon de Valéra had no choice. Neutrality included denying Britain the use of 'treaty ports' that she had only recently vacated. With these bases, the RAF could have extended its protection of Atlantic convoys over a wider radius, and some lives and ships would certainly have been saved. British anger over this is probably the origin of stories that Eire was refuelling U-boats in sheltered areas of its west coast.

In 1939 Eire had negligible stocks of the type of diesel U-boats used, and she suffered from a chronic shortage of fuel of all kinds throughout the war. The idea that Ireland would give fuel to Germany to sink Allied shipping – a major source of what little oil did arrive in the country – is absurd. You would also expect documentary evidence or eyewitness accounts of U-boats in Ireland to have emerged by now. There are no papers, and no U-boat crewman has ever come forward to claim his vessel refuelled in Ireland, while plenty have spoken of refuelling in Spain, another ostensibly neutral country. U-boats did operate near the Irish coast, though this was hazardous because of British bases in Ulster. One surfaced near Dingle in October 1939 to land the crew of a Greek merchant vessel it had sunk. Others probably entered Irish territorial waters from time to time, but certainly without the collusion of de Valéra's government. *Eugene Byrne*

Why was the British Brown Bess musket such a formidable weapon?

The Brown Bess was one of the outstanding infantry weapons of all time. The earliest models entered service with the British Army at the turn of the 18th century, and later versions remained the weapon of choice as late as 1840. The musket was loaded through the muzzle from a pre-packed cartridge. This enabled the soldier to keep his powder dry and to load quickly. The Brown Bess achieved a misfire rate as low as 12 per cent, while it could be fired every 20 seconds or so. Both features were great improvements on older weapons. The flintlock firing mechanism was also perfectly safe –

10 Fighting females

Women who pretended to be men to serve as soldiers.

1 **Christian Davies**
Scots Greys, French Wars,
c.1695–1706

2 **Mary Ralphson**
King's Own Dragoons, War of
Austrian Succession, 1743–6

3 **Phoebe Hessel**
5th Foot, Fontenoy,
1745

4 **Hannah Snell**
Fraser's Marines, Siege of
Pondicherry, 1748

5 **Deborah Samson**
4th US Massachusetts Regiment,
American War of Independence,
1782–3

6 **Mary Anne Talbot**
82nd Foot, Revolutionary Wars,
1792–6

7 **Nadezhda Durova**
Russian Cavalry, Napoleonic
Wars, 1806–14

8 **Elizabeth Hatzler**
French Dragoons, Invasion of
Russia, 1812

9 **Sarah Wakeman**
153rd New York Volunteers,
American Civil War, 1862–4

10 **Cathay Williams**
38th US Infantry,
American West,
1866–8

whereas the older matchlock had scattered sparks at random. Consequently, musketeers could form up shoulder to shoulder without danger to each other, enabling the firing of massed volleys of gunfire.

The weapon was largely inaccurate beyond 90 metres (100 yards), but what gave it the edge in battle was the training of the soldiers. The British infantry trained in firing their guns rapidly and reliably more than any other European army. Moreover, the adoption of a line two or three men deep meant that each man could fire his weapon at the enemy. Other armies retained formations four or more ranks deep. This added momentum to a charge and was easier for raw recruits to maintain, but meant that the rear ranks could not fire their guns.

The name 'Brown Bess' derived from a chemical coating to the barrels that resisted rust. The coating was dropped after about 1740, but the name stuck. *Rupert Matthews*

Did you know...?

The youngest US serviceman to fight in the Second World War was 12 years old. Calvin Graham lied about his age to enlist in the navy. He was wounded and won the Purple Heart, but was given a dishonourable discharge after his mother revealed his true age.
Nick Rennison

I found a Second World War gas mask in my attic. If Britain had suffered gas attacks, would it have been any good? And is it worth any money?

The masks that were distributed on the Home Front came in four models (infant, child, civilian and civilian service) and used an air filter of cotton wool and 'activated charcoal', which was highly porous, with a huge surface area to trap gas particles. Civilian respirators would not have been as effective as military ones, but it was reasonable to assume that there would be higher concentrations of gas on a battlefield. Assuming people were given sufficient warning of an attack, the masks would have been very effective against non-persistent gases, such as chlorine, and would have offered a high degree of protection against the effects of mustard gas on the eyes and lungs.

It could be argued that the masks were very successful in deterring Hitler from using gas because none was ever deployed. A more pressing reason for not using it, though, was that German civilians were not issued with masks because of the difficulties Germany had in obtaining rubber, which is essential for an airtight seal around the face. The Allies also made it clear that they would retaliate if Germany resorted to 'first use'. As for value...some 8 million masks were handed out in Britain, and the government didn't bother collecting them back. The best recent price for a UK Second World War (adult) civilian respirator on eBay was £10.95.
Eugene Byrne

Two sorts of air raid shelter were issued in the Second World War – the Anderson and the Morrison. Who were Anderson and Morrison?

One and a half million Anderson shelters, with the capacity to protect several million people, had been issued by the beginning of the Second World War. These corrugated iron air raid shelters, erected in gardens, were named after Sir John Anderson, the Lord Privy Seal, who had responsibility for Air Raid Precautions (ARP). Anderson was originally a civil servant, and had been involved in planning since the 1920s. During the war he became home secretary and minister for home security, moving on to become Lord President; he remained essentially a highly successful non-party bureaucrat.

Anderson's successor as home secretary was the Labour politician Herbert Morrison, who introduced the indoor shelter named after him in March 1941. These large, table-like steel cages, 2 metres (6½ feet) long, 1.2 metres (4 feet) wide, and 85 centimetres (2¾ feet) high, were more popular than the Anderson shelter because people did not have to go outside to use them when the siren sounded. Morrison was one of the most successful Labour members of Churchill's coalition government, and went on to become Lord President and Leader of the Commons, and briefly foreign secretary in Attlee's Labour government of 1945–51. *Gary Sheffield*

How was the Unknown Soldier, who is buried in Westminster Abbey, chosen?

The grave of the Unknown Soldier or Warrior is a symbolic memorial to all the British and Commonwealth dead of the First World War, particularly those without a known grave. He was buried in Westminster Abbey on Armistice Day 1920. The body was chosen from four unidentified servicemen exhumed from cemeteries in four battle areas (the Aisne, the Somme, Ypres and Arras). The bodies, draped in Union flags, were laid out in a chapel in northern France and Brigadier General L.J. Wyatt, then the general officer in charge of troops in France and Flanders, selected one of them to be the Unknown Warrior. The others were returned to their graves. *Nick Rennison*

Wish I hadn't said that...

'I believe it is peace for our time.'

Neville Chamberlain, British prime minister, 30 September 1938, following the Munich Agreement. Less than a year later Britain was at war with Germany.

I've been told that the longbow was a more accurate weapon than the musket, and had a higher rate of shooting. If this is so, why did the musketeer replace the archer on the battlefield?

On the surface, this is indeed a puzzle. A skilled longbow man could shoot ten arrows a minute, while even the most adept musket-bearing infantryman of the Napoleonic period would struggle to fire more than two rounds in that time. Moreover, whereas the effective range of a musket could be as little as 45 metres (50 yards), an archer could fire with reasonable accuracy up to 270 metres (300 yards). To become a proficient archer, however, took a great deal of practice, while it was generally a relatively straightforward matter to teach a man the few simple drills required to load, stand in line, point the musket in the general direction of the enemy, and fire. This meant that large bodies of men could quickly be turned into effective soldiers, which was of great importance when the size of armies began to grow from the 16th century onwards. As armies became much larger, they relied on the mass effect of musketry and cannon-fire, and the skilled archer became a redundant luxury. *Gary Sheffield*

If Wellington had lost at Waterloo, would Napoleon finally have won the Napoleonic Wars?

Had Napoleon won at Waterloo, he would only have disposed of one of several enemy armies. Blucher's Prussians also fought in the campaign, and Russia and Austria were mobilising forces. The sheer numbers of the allied troops would probably have prevailed in the end. Napoleon's only real hope of ultimate victory was to split the coalition ranged against him, but this too seems unlikely. The emperor's enemies had learnt that his ambition was insatiable. After defeating him in 1814, Napoleon had been treated relatively mildly, condemned to exile in Elba. He escaped less than a year later and, on his return to France, dethroned Louis XVIII, placing himself once again at odds with the allies grouped against him. In March 1815 the allies signed a treaty declaring Napoleon an outlaw, and formed a coalition to defeat him once and for all. Barring a series of victories, crushing even by Napoleon's standards, French victory at Waterloo would probably only have postponed the final overthrow of Napoleonic France. *Gary Sheffield*

Wish I hadn't said that...

'Hitler has missed the bus.'

British prime minister Neville Chamberlain, 5 April 1940.
Four days later the Germans began their conquest of Norway
and Denmark.

In which war were the most animals killed, proportionately?

Very tricky! If you mean animals directly employed by the combatants, it could well be the American Civil War, which saw industrialisation producing death on a vast scale. The population of the Union and Confederate States was around 31 million, and various sources estimate that 1–1.5 million horses, mules and donkeys died in the conflict (along with over 620,000 human beings). An estimated 8 million horses died in the First World War. Proportionately, this conflict was less deadly than the American Civil War as around half the world's population of 1.3 billion were involved in the conflict. In fact, more horses may have died at the end of the war when they became redundant and, as a result, were slaughtered in their thousands.

Animals were still being used in the Second World War, from the tens of thousands of carrier-pigeons that took messages from resistance groups in occupied Europe to the pack-mules (with their vocal cords cut to prevent them making noise) used by the British in the Burmese jungle

The Thirty Years War (1618–48) would be a strong contender for the war causing the largest proportionate number of animal deaths. Over a fifth of the estimated 20 million human population of Germany and Central Europe died, mostly of disease and starvation, and when people are starving, not even the rats stand a chance.

The most recent conflict with a high proportion of animal deaths is almost certainly the Vietnam War. Livestock and wildlife died in huge numbers as a result of imprecise area-bombing, booby-traps and landmines. The Americans also used powerful herbicides, most notoriously Agent Orange, to destroy vast areas of forest in an attempt to deny the insurgents jungle cover. Around 1.5 million hectares (3.75 million acres) – 10 per cent of South Vietnam – were sprayed, destroying entire ecosystems, many of which have still not recovered. *Eugene Byrne*

Did you know…?

In the 1870s Paraguay briefly legalised polygamy. During the War of the Triple Alliance (1864–70) so many Paraguayan soldiers had been killed that the country had vastly more women than men. The legislation was intended to help the population to recover.
Nick Rennison

Would the trench warfare on the Western Front in the First World War have existed if the machine gun had not been invented until the 1920s?

Trenches of the kind established on the Western Front were essentially the consequence of the abrupt change at the end of 1914 from mobile to static warfare. When the initial German offensive stalled and both sides hurried north in the 'race to the sea', it was evident that there would be a showdown battle. If the Germans won, this could have ended the war; if they failed, with all the armies involved depleted by massive losses and in a state of exhaustion, the outcome would be stalemate. Effectively, both sides would be stranded where the fighting stopped. In view of this you couldn't camp out cheerfully in the open and wait for the next season. The only response was to dig holes on the ground as quickly as possible and get into them. These holes eventually linked to form a double line of trenches running 720 kilometres (450 miles) from the Channel to Switzerland. The British Commander-in-Chief, Field Marshal Sir John French, had foreseen this possibility back in October during a brief period of static warfare; in such conditions, he wrote 'the spade will be as great a necessity as the rifle'.

Digging trenches did not depend on the presence of machine guns. Contrary to popular opinion, it was artillery that would prove to be the greatest killing weapon of the war. From the start, too, the closeness of the trenches offered an open invitation for the sniper to practise his traditional deadly skills. A sinister ritual soon developed, known as 'the sniper's kiss' – the bid by an expert practitioner to effect a last killing on the edge of nightfall. There was only one brief respite from this, on Christmas Eve before the famous truce.

When we think of the machine gun we of course remember such massacres as the first day of the Somme, but trenches were there long before Britain's finest went over the top on 1 July 1916, and the war of the Western Front would have followed much the same scenario had machine guns been only a pipe dream for the future. *Malcolm Brown*

I watched the Fleet Review at Portsmouth and was struck by the fact that navies no longer have battleships. Why is this, and when was Britain's last battleship scrapped?

Battleships – large, heavily armoured warships equipped with heavy guns – were eclipsed during the Second World War by aircraft carriers. The great naval battles in the Pacific were decided by aircraft, not by conventional surface battles. The loss of battleships, such as *Bismarck* in 1941, seemed to underline the vulnerability of this type of warship. But it is worth noting that battleships still had a role to play in naval warfare and were difficult to sink. *Bismarck* took an enormous amount of punishment, including air attack and naval gunfire.

The advent of the nuclear age caused a reassessment of the role of navies, but battleships underwent a renaissance in the late cold war. During the 1980s, several US battleships were reactivated and saw service in the 1991 Gulf War, but were later stood down. The 1980s' Soviet Kirov class of nuclear heavy cruisers looked remarkably like a new generation of battleships. But battleships are costly to maintain, very labour intensive in requiring large crews, and offer less operational flexibility than aircraft carriers.

The last of the Royal Navy's battleships was HMS *Vanguard*, which was launched in 1944, but only entered service in 1946. *Vanguard* was decommissioned in 1954 without having been in action, and the ship was finally scrapped in 1960. Since the 1950s, the Royal Navy has found the battleship an unaffordable luxury.
Gary Sheffield

I've heard that a regiment of the British Army served as Pontius Pilate's bodyguard. Where does this legend come from?

The Royal Scots, the First of Foot, ranks as the senior infantry regiment of the line (that is, excluding the Foot Guards). It is one of the oldest regiments in the British Army. Formed in 1633, it served in the Swedish army of Gustavus Adolphus, and came into English service during the reign of Charles II, when the regular standing army was raised.

For many years the regiment has been nicknamed 'Pontius Pilate's Bodyguard', an allusion to its antiquity. In the time-honoured fashion of old soldiers telling tall tales, elaborate stories were fabricated about the regiment being on duty during the

Crucifixion! In fact, the Buffs (East Kent Regiment), who were numbered in the order of precedence as 3rd Foot, are even older than the Royal Scots, having been raised in 1572 for service in the Netherlands. *Gary Sheffield*

What happened to the fleet Julius Caesar used for his first attempted invasion of Britain?

The warships of ancient Rome were not masterpieces of naval engineering. They were designed for Mediterranean use, where they stayed in harbour during rough weather and could be hauled on to beaches if a sudden storm appeared. They never went far from land, and were quite unsuitable for use in northern waters. Various technical clues in the writings of Caesar suggest that his men built ships of the type generally termed 'Liburnian'. These were oared galleys some 35 metres (115 feet) long and 4 metres (13 feet) in the beam. They were powered by 120 rowers, each pulling a separate oar, and were steered by a pair of extra large oars at the rear. These ships were built of thin planks of pine or fir, as speed in battle was paramount. The Roman craft were used for the expedition of 55 BC, and most were smashed by a storm on the southern coast of Britain. It was this sudden lack of ships, and thus supplies, that forced Caesar to call off his campaign and hurry back to Gaul.

By contrast, the local Celts built very different ships. These were around 20 metres (65 feet) long and 6 metres (20 feet) broad, and were built of stout oak timbers and planking. They were designed for use in rough seas, far from land. Caesar hired and conscripted several such ships from the tribes of northern Gaul for his second expedition of 54 BC, and did rather better. After this campaign the Celtic ships were returned to their owners. Although Caesar does not say what happened to the Roman-built galleys, it must be assumed that they were broken up or left to rot, having proved unsuitable for use in the Channel and North Sea. *Rupert Matthews*

Wish I hadn't said that...

'Well, gentlemen, it might be worse...it might be raining.'
General Sir William Slim on the retreat from Burma, April 1942.
Two hours later it was raining. Hard.

When was the explosive shell first used?

Gunpowder weapons were being used in China during the 12th century; a carving of 1128 in a temple shows a primitive artillery piece in use. Artillery was employed in the West by the 14th century, the first-known picture dating from 1327. Then, as now, it fell into two broad types: hand guns, which were more or less portable, and larger, crew-served weapons, usually used as siege weapons. At this stage guns fired solid projectiles. The famous 'Mons Meg', manufactured in 1449 and now on display at Edinburgh Castle, hurled a 45-centimetre (18-inch) ball made of granite.

It seems that some attempt to develop the ancestor of the explosive shell was made towards the end of the 1300s. Explosive material was placed in a hollow iron projectile and ignited by a fuse. However, it was not until the 16th and 17th centuries that explosive shells became more common. Further developments include the work of a British officer, Henry Shrapnel (1761–1842), who gave his name to an anti-personnel explosive shell equipped with a fuse that threw out musket balls with devastating effects on anyone caught within range. The predecessors of modern high-explosive shells, based on steel and TNT and employing clockwork fuses, were developed during the 19th century. *Gary Sheffield*

10 Tommy slang words

During the First World War, new recruits could get into a lot of trouble if they didn't know the lingo...

1 **Axle grease**
butter

2 **Battle bowler**
steel helmet

3 **Canteen medals**
beer stains on a tunic

4 **Cold meat ticket**
identity disc

5 **Donkey walloper**
cavalryman

6 **Duckboard harrier**
runner or messenger

7 **Jack Johnson**
large German shell

8 **Knee drill**
church parade

9 **Linseed lancers**
Royal Army Medical Corps

10 **Short arm inspection**
medical examination for VD

A letter written from New Zealand by my great-great-aunt in March 1904 reads: 'See that the *Mongolia* by which we are returning to England was fired at and chased by a Russian warship in the Red Sea.' Is this true?

Unfortunately, the log of the steam packet *Mongolia* cannot be found, but the event is not implausible. In February 1904 war broke out between Japan and Russia. The conflict followed years of tension as the two countries squabbled over lands and influence in the northern parts of the crumbling Chinese Empire. Fighting began on 8 February 1904, when the Japanese launched a surprise attack on the Russian naval base of Port Arthur (Lüshkunou). At the time Britain and Japan had a defensive alliance. Although Britain did not join the war, as the Japanese had attacked first, the Russians were understandably wary of British ships. The *Mongolia* was lucky to have escaped. Other British craft were less lucky. The most notorious incident took place on 21 October 1904, when Russian warships in the North Sea mistook British trawlers for Japanese torpedo boats and opened fire, killing several men. *Rupert Matthews*

Who was the last British king to command troops in battle? Have 20th-century royals fought in battles?

At the Battle of Dettingen, fought against the French in 1743 during the War of the Austrian Succession, George II personally commanded British and Hanoverian troops. He was the last serving British monarch to carry out this role on the battlefield. However, Prince Albert (the future George VI) fought with the Royal Navy on board HMS *Collingwood* at Jutland in 1916. His brother, the Prince of Wales, later King Edward VIII, served with the army on the Western Front, but was confined to a staff officer's post and forbidden to serve in the trenches. A number of royals have been in action in the previous century. Prince Philip was a naval officer in the Second World War. Serving on HMS *Valiant* at the battle of Matapan in 1941, he was mentioned in dispatches for controlling the battleship's searchlights. His son, Prince Andrew, served as a helicopter pilot during the 1982 Falklands War. Prince Harry is the latest royal to continue the family tradition, having seen active service in Afghanistan. *Gary Sheffield*

Wish I hadn't said that…

'Wellington is a bad general, the English are bad troops, and this affair is nothing more serious than eating one's breakfast.'

Napoleon Bonaparte to his generals on the morning of the Battle of Waterloo, June 1815.

Hitler's V-1 and V-2 weapons are well known, but I've heard there was also a V-3 that was never used. Can you tell me more about this?

Unlike the V-1, which was a primitive cruise missile, and the V-2, a ballistic missile, the V-3 was a collection of huge guns. The remains of the V-3 site, built by slave labourers who paid a terrible price, can be seen at Mimoyecques in northern France. Although it was never completed, the V-3 was intended to consist of 50 artillery tubes spread across two sites. Each barrel was approximately 145 metres (490 feet) long, and fired 15-centimetre (6-inch) shells propelled by explosive charges. The threat was ominous: had the V-3 sites become fully operational, London could have been bombarded with up to ten shells every minute. Although construction began in 1943, the V-3 was never properly completed, and initial tests demonstrated a number of teething problems. Moreover, the Allies carried out a number of air strikes on the V-3 sites. In July 1944 RAF bombers used Tallboy bombs, designed to pierce thick concrete. The raid caused considerable destruction, killing many workers in the complex. The site was captured in late August 1944 by Allied troops advancing along the French coast. *Gary Sheffield*

Is it true that the world came closer to nuclear war in 1983 than at any time since the Cuban Missile Crisis?

The 'new cold war' of the early 1980s was one of the most dangerous phases of the struggle between the USA and USSR. The Soviet invasion of Afghanistan in 1979 caused great alarm in the West. The Kremlin was just as worried by the hawkish policies of US president Ronald Reagan. By late 1983 relations were at rock bottom. Incidents such as Reagan's announcement of the Star

Wars SDI anti-missile programme, the American invasion of Grenada, and the shooting down of a Korean airliner by the Soviets, who claimed that it had been spying, contributed to the air of crisis. In November 1983 NATO forces held an exercise codenamed Able Archer 83. The frantically worried Soviet leadership believed that this war game might be the cover for a real nuclear attack. Meanwhile, Western powers feared that the USSR might pre-empt with a nuclear strike of its own. Fortunately, a KGB double agent informed the West of Soviet alarm, and the danger passed. The crisis led to Reagan toning down his rhetoric, and in 1984 superpower relations began to improve. *Gary Sheffield*

In the Second World War why did Japan ally itself with Adolf Hitler, whose Aryan supremacist philosophy and contempt for other races were well known?

Strangely, Adolf Hitler largely exempted the Japanese from his hatred of non-Aryan races. In the words of the American historian Gerhard Weinberg, he saw them as 'very clever' and 'their aggressive moves in the Far East, which brought down upon them the attacks of the liberal press, were to their credit in Hitler's eyes'. There was an obvious ideological affinity between Nazi Germany and authoritarian, militarist Japan, and cooperation suited both states. In the 1930s both Germany and Japan were 'have not' powers that sought to change the international situation in their favour by aggression. If Japan was to get involved in a colonial war with Britain and France, this would obviously benefit German plans in Europe. Japan might also serve to hold the United States in check. Likewise, Japan gained a huge advantage by the defeat of France in 1940, which enabled the Japanese to move into French possessions in the Far East without war. In 1941–2 the response of Britain – embroiled in a war with Germany and Italy – to the Japanese offensive in East Asia was feeble. The German–Japanese alliance was very much a marriage of convenience, and there were frequent clashes of interest. It is possible that had Germany and Japan achieved total victory, the two new superpowers would then have turned on each other. *Gary Sheffield*

Why were some British soldiers in the First World War known as the Old Contemptibles?

The first British soldiers to land in France in 1914 were members of the British Expeditionary Force. The German Kaiser, Wilhelm II, had supposedly called them 'a contemptible little army', and the soldiers transformed the insult into a badge of pride by referring to themselves as the Old Contemptibles. *Nick Rennison*

During the Second World War, was the US mainland ever directly attacked by the Germans or the Japanese?

In February 1942 a Japanese submarine shelled an oil refinery near Santa Barbara in California, and six months later a seaplane flew over Oregon, dropping incendiary bombs in an over-optimistic attempt to start large-scale forest fires. Late in the war the Japanese launched thousands of bomb-laden balloons in the general direction of America. A few hundred reached the USA, and six people were killed when one of them exploded. These were the only deaths to occur on the US mainland due to enemy action during the whole of the war. *Nick Rennison*

I have heard that the army rank of field marshal was recently abolished. Is this true, and who was the last to be appointed?

The rank of field marshal, which dates back to at least the 18th century, has not been formally abolished. However, the independent Betts Report of 1995 recommended that no further appointments should be made to this rank, or its naval and RAF equivalents, admiral of the fleet and marshal of the Royal Air Force. The reason given was that the size of the British armed services no longer warranted 'five star' rank, but it was widely believed within the forces that the Ministry of Defence acted upon this recommendation (on 20 February 1996) as a money-saving measure. Only should a major war occur, or some other unforeseen circumstance happen, would the rank be resurrected.

The last serving officer to be promoted to field marshal was the then Sir Peter Inge, in March 1994. Historically, however, the rank has been awarded not only to distinguished soldiers, but also to British and foreign royalty. Thus HRH Prince Philip, the Duke of Edinburgh, although a career naval officer, was appointed as a field marshal in 1953, and the Duke of Kent was similarly honoured in 1993. The late King of Nepal was an honorary field marshal, and previous foreign royalty to be given this rank included Kaiser Wilhelm II of Germany and Emperor Hirohito of Japan. It remains to be seen whether there will be any future royal field marshals. *Gary Sheffield*

Churchill once said, 'History is written by the victors.' Are there any parts of the official historical record that are thought to be not fully representative of the truth?

All history is written from the viewpoint and with the prejudices of the writer. The fact that the victors of any war or political struggle tend to have access to the means of preserving their version of events does indeed mean that their accounts are more likely to survive. It is sometimes possible for modern historians to peek behind these official accounts to discover a hidden reality – and there must be many instances of a victor's falsehoods that have yet to be unmasked. In *c*.1275 BC, for instance, the Egyptian pharaoh Rameses II fought the Battle of Kadesh against the Hittite Empire. According to the account carved on temple walls by Rameses, the battle was a stunning Egyptian victory due largely to his own skills. That this was not the case is shown by the fact that the war dragged on until *c*.1258 BC, when a treaty was signed in which Rameses agreed to respect Hittite borders and not to try to tempt Hittite allies to the Egyptian cause.

More subtle are the distortions in the formal account of the Battle of El Alamein in 1942. This was undoubtedly a great victory for the British 8th Army under General Montgomery over Germany's Afrika Korps led by General Rommel. At the time, and for years afterwards, Montgomery claimed that the battle had been fought entirely to plan, thus boosting his reputation as a superlative military planner. When the military records were opened to historians, however, it was revealed that Montgomery had radically changed his plans in mid-battle when German resistance turned out to be stronger than anticipated. Thus Montgomery was shown to have been a superb improviser rather than a good planner. Why he should have sought to hide one skill behind another in this way is unclear. Other examples are too numerous to mention. No doubt readers will have their favourites. *Rupert Matthews*

What was the last battle fought on English soil?

Some reference works describe the Battle of Sedgemoor in 1685 as the last battle fought on English soil. It was certainly the last major engagement, but both Jacobite Rebellions (in 1715 and 1745) saw opposing troops confront one another in England. Thus, the last battle in England took place at Clifton Moor near Penrith on 18 December 1745, between Hanoverian soldiers and Bonnie Prince Charlie's men as the latter retreated to Scotland. The last battle in Great Britain was the far more famous encounter at Culloden the following April. *Nick Rennison*

What was the Pottawatomie Massacre?

The Pottawatomie Massacre is a name given to one of the bloody events in Kansas in the years preceding the American Civil War. On 24 May 1856 John Brown (the man whose body famously lies a-mouldering in the grave while his soul goes marching on) led a group of his anti-slavery followers into a township of pro-slavery settlers near the Pottawatomie Creek in Kansas. Five of the settlers were killed in cold blood. The massacre took place more than three years before the famous events at Harpers Ferry – Brown's attempt to start an armed slave revolt. This resulted in the trial and execution of John Brown. *Nick Rennison*

Was French time in 1918 one hour ahead of British time as it is today? If so, was the ceasefire for the end of the First World War at 11 o'clock British time or French time?

No war ended so precisely as the Great War: following agreements signed in Marshal Foch's railway train at Compiègne earlier that day, the four-year-long holocaust was scheduled to end at 11 a.m. on 11 November 1918. Had the present differentiation between British and French time applied, this would have meant the ceasefire in France taking place one hour ahead of the expected celebrations in Britain, while boats criss-crossing the Channel would have found themselves traversing a freak kind of international date-line between peace and war. Happily, this was not the case. British and French time was synchronised. So when, at 11 o'clock, Big Ben proclaimed the end of hostilities over London, the same message boomed from the steeples of France and

Belgium. For Germany it was different. The Armistice did not take effect until 12 noon. But in the case of the Western Allies who had fought together, they were able to lay down their arms simultaneously.

Reactions were many and various. Some Allied units were furious that a successful advance had been stopped. In other cases, there was sheer relief that the slaughter was over. My own favourite story is that told by a Major R.S. Cockburn of the 63rd (Royal Naval) Division, whose battalion, he claimed, was 'probably nearer to Berlin than any other British troops'. For him the news of the Armistice was 'as if the sun had forced its way through a bank of cloud', though 'on the whole the men took the news philosophically. One of them said to me, "Well, that is a good thing, sir, isn't it?"' This must surely qualify as one of the great understatements of the day, if not of the whole war.
Malcolm Brown

In the days of National Service how long would an immigrant have had to be a British citizen to be called up? Were any exempt?

The National Service Act of 1947 effectively continued the conscription of men into the armed forces that had begun in 1939. To the public the call-up in wartime was known as conscription. In peacetime it was designated as National Service.

Under National Service, young men had to serve 18 months in the armed forces, and then four years in the reserves, generally in the Territorial Army. The call-up could come at any time between the ages of 18 and 26, a fact that was resented by many men who were starting a career and would have preferred to do their time when it suited them, rather than when it suited the government. Due to the pressure on the armed forces during the Korean War, the period of National Service was increased to two years in 1950, the time in the reserves being reduced to compensate. All able-bodied male British citizens were liable to be called up, whether they were born in Britain or overseas. The only exceptions were men working in one of three reserved occupations: coal mining, agriculture or the merchant navy. Neither foreign nationals living in Britain nor non-British citizens living in the empire were called up.
Rupert Matthews

How did the Japanese and German governments correspond during the Second World War?

The idea of governments picking up the phone to one another is of very modern provenance. During the Second World War communications between Berlin and Tokyo were made through the usual diplomatic channels; Berlin, therefore, would communicate with Tokyo via its embassy in the Japanese capital, while Tokyo would correspond with the Nazi government through its Berlin-based ambassador. Naturally, given the sensitivity of those transmissions, secure communication systems were absolutely essential. To this end, the Germans had developed the famous Enigma machine, and the Japanese had the analogous Type B cipher. Both worked in broadly the same way, transforming inputted text into randomised code that could be sent by cable or radio, and could be deciphered only through an identical machine using the correct settings. So even if the messages were intercepted, the logic ran, the codes would never be broken.

However, neither of these systems was entirely secure. The British successes with breaking Enigma codes are well documented, but it is less common knowledge that the Japanese Type B system had also been broken. American cryptologists in 1940 had already succeeded in breaking the Japanese code, and it was a technique that they shared with the British. So, from early 1941 onwards, Japanese signals traffic in and out of Berlin was regularly being deciphered by the Allies. Intelligence was gleaned from this source, but although the Germans and Japanese were allies, the degree of strategic cooperation – and therefore of secret sharing – between them was minimal. *Roger Moorhouse*

Did Boudicca really ride into battle in a chariot with scythes attached to its wheels, as depicted in the history picture books of my childhood?

Scythed chariots did exist in the ancient world, but there is only a single doubtful reference to ancient Britons riding them, and no evidence that Boudicca used one. The image of the queen in her scythed chariot, which we all know, was created in the Victorian era and had its finest expression in the statue of her by Thomas Thornycroft, which stands by the Thames at Westminster.
Nick Rennison

Wish I hadn't said that...

'They couldn't hit an elephant at this distance.'

Union General John Sedgwick, shortly before being shot by a sniper at Spotsylvania, May 1864.

Under what circumstances were prisoners of war repatriated at the end of the Second World War?

Although liberation and repatriation were what all POWs had most desired, the often-chaotic reality of the end of the war was nonetheless a challenge for many of them. Initially, former prisoners would be sorted and classified by their liberators before being moved to transit camps, where medical care would be provided. From there they would be repatriated, in most cases to their home countries.

It was often when former POWs arrived home, however, that the first problems arose. Many were profoundly affected by their experiences and had tremendous difficulty in returning to everyday life. After the initial euphoria, there was often a corrosive sense of anti-climax and a feeling that they were not understood or valued. A proportion of POWs had deeper problems. Some were thoroughly institutionalised and unable to adjust to life 'on the outside'; others had problems with depression, with authority, with women, or with the wider challenges of 're-socialisation'. Those returning from the Far East often bore the mental scars of years of torture and abuse.

The British response to such challenges was surprisingly enlightened. Civil Resettlement Units (CRUs) were set up, with psychiatrists, doctors and therapists on hand, to provide a haven for ex-POWs and to ease their reintegration into society. However, in the vast majority of cases, such assistance was ignored. Only 6 per cent of POWs attended the voluntary CRUs; the remainder simply did the best they could, suffering in silence. In addition, no extra provision was made for those ex-prisoners of the Japanese whose psychological problems were often more acute. Civilian ex-prisoners, moreover, fell through the net entirely. For such people, it was assumed that time and a dose of 'stiff upper lip' would provide a cure for all ills. Sadly, they did not. *Roger Moorhouse*

Could you tell me which nation had the first-known spies?

By their very nature, spies are secretive and underhand. Most governments will deny that they employ or use spies – even when they are caught red-handed doing just that. It can therefore be difficult to judge when a scout becomes a spy. Around 720 BC the Assyrians had a unit of elite soldiers called the Quradu. These men formed a personal bodyguard for the king, but were also sent on secretive special missions that took them away from Assyria for extended periods. They might well have been spying in enemy lands. Almost as obscure are the activities of the Spartan unit known as the Krypteia (the Hidden Ones), who were active from about 600 BC to 200 BC. These men were chosen for their skills at night work and camouflage. Again, it is thought that they acted as spies, but their work might have been more in the way of reconnaissance.

One of the earliest explicit references to spies comes in the works of the Greek historian Herodotus, when he was writing about the build-up to the Persian invasion of Greece in 480 BC. The Greeks, he tells us, sent spies to the area around Sardis (now in modern-day Turkey) where the Persian army was gathering. These spies were caught, but instead of executing them, the Persian emperor Xerxes sent them on a guided tour of his forces. Xerxes wanted the Greeks to know the vast force he was leading in the hope of cowing them into surrender. Herodotus shows no surprise that spies had been sent, only at Xerxes' reaction. We can only assume that by this date spies were commonplace and spying was widely practised, even though there is little mention in the written record. *Rupert Matthews*

During the Second World War, how did the Germans treat Commonwealth War Graves from the First World War?

This is a subject that is still loaded with mythology. The truth is that the Germans showed considerable respect to Commonwealth War Graves from the First World War, for the simple fact that the German dead from that conflict were just as sacred to them as the Allied dead were to the British and French. This was underlined in 1940, when Hitler himself paid his respects at the German

cemetery at Langemarck in Flanders. En route he also visited the
Canadian memorial at Vimy to disprove Allied claims that
cemeteries were being desecrated by German troops. The root of
those claims was the few instances where Germans did demolish
monuments. This occurred when the wording or imagery was
considered offensive, a famous example being the memorial to the
Second Australian Division at Mont St Quentin, which featured a
statue of a soldier bayoneting a German eagle. Otherwise, Allied
cemeteries were left well alone. There is even a tale of a downed
RAF airman hiding in a cemetery gardener's hut because he knew
the Germans would never look for him there. *Roger Moorhouse*

Why did American paratroopers shout 'Geronimo' when they jumped from their planes?

The troops testing the feasibility of mass parachute drops at Fort
Benning, Georgia, in 1940 were shown movies to entertain them
off duty. The night before a particularly stressful test jump the men
watched a Paramount B-movie about the cavalry and Apaches
entitled *Geronimo*. A trooper named Aubrey Eberhardt told his
fellows that he would relieve the tension the following morning by
yelling 'Geronimo' as he jumped. He did so and the cry soon
spread to all US airborne troops. *Nick Rennison*

Why do many First World War memorials have the dates 1914–1919 on them?

Famously, the First World War is said to have ended on the 11th
hour of the 11th day of the 11th month of 1918. Although the
fighting on the Western Front certainly ceased (at least in most
areas) at this time, the Armistice that came into effect at 11 a.m.
on 11 November 1918 was a truce, not the definitive end of the
conflict. The war between the Allies and Germany did not formally
end until the signing of the Treaty of Versailles on 28 June 1919.
During the negotiations, the Germans were aware that if they held
out against the harsh terms stipulated, the Allies (in theory,
although probably not in practice) could have recommenced
military operations.

Technically, the First World War went on even after peace was
signed in Paris, as separate treaties were concluded with

Germany's allies. The peace of Trianon, with Hungary, was not signed until June 1920. Peace with the Ottoman Empire was agreed at Sèvres in October 1920, but the emergence of the Turkish republic from the wreck of the empire necessitated a new treaty (of Lausanne) in 1923.

Despite the end of the war with the Central Powers, many British troops remained on active service long after the Armistice. British forces were committed to Russia in a failed attempt to crush Lenin's Communist regime; an increasingly bitter (and ultimately unsuccessful) counter-insurgency campaign was fought in Ireland; and occupation duties in places such as Egypt and Iraq were far from peaceful. *Gary Sheffield*

It's common knowledge that the plane that dropped the atomic bomb on Hiroshima was called the *Enola Gay*, but what was the name of the aircraft that bombed Nagasaki?

The B-29 American bomber that dropped the nuclear weapon on Nagasaki was called *Bockscar*. Usually flown by a pilot named Frederick Bock, *Bockscar* was captained on its atomic mission by Major Charles Sweeney. The target for the bomb, originally the city of Kokura, was changed at the last minute because of cloud cover obscuring it. As he had been ordered to chart the descent of the bomb visually, Sweeney chose to fly on to Nagasaki, where the clouds had cleared. *Nick Rennison*

I read on a visit to Prague that the Thirty Years War was precipitated by the Second Defenestration of Prague. Can you shed any light on the First Defenestration?

The 1618 Defenestration (the act of throwing someone out of a window), also known as the Second Defenestration of Prague, was a major catalyst in the outbreak of the Thirty Years War. It was a reaction to a cessation in the building of a Protestant chapel on lands owned by the Catholic clergy. Protestants interpreted the cessation order as a violation of the right to freedom of religious expression granted in the Letter of Majesty, issued by Emperor Rudolf II in 1609. They also feared that his successor Ferdinand II would revoke the Protestant rights altogether once he came to the throne.

At Prague Castle on 23 May 1618 an assembly of Protestants, led by Count Thurn, tried two imperial governors, Vilem Slavata of Chlum (1572–1652) and Jaroslav Borzita of Martinice (1582–1649), for violating the Letter of Majesty (Right of Freedom of Religion), found them guilty, and threw them, together with their scribe Philip Fabricius, out of the windows of the Bohemian Chancellery. The First Defenestration occurred in 1419, during a time of unrest between the Catholic establishment and the followers of religious reformer Jan Hus. After his death the Hussites, as they became known, continued to campaign for religious reform, and in 1419 a group of them stormed the New Town Hall in Prague and threw several members of the town council out of the windows. This event also precipitated a war – the Hussite Wars, 1419–c.1437.

There may also have been a Third Defenestration – projecting unpopular leaders from windows being an apparently favoured form of assassination in Czech history – in March 1948, when minister Jan Masaryk was found dead underneath his bathroom window. *Steph Gapper*

When was the last time a British cavalry regiment made a charge in anger during a battle?

The last charge made by British cavalry at a regimental level seems to have taken place at El Mughar in Palestine on 13 November 1917, when the Royal Buckinghamshire Hussars, supported by the Dorset and Berkshire Yeomanry, overran a Turkish position, taking several hundred prisoners. However, this was not the last time a British cavalry force charged 'in anger'. On 11 November 1918, minutes before the Armistice brought fighting to an end, a squadron of the 7th Dragoon Guards charged into the Belgian town of Lessines, which was held by the Germans, and seized the crossings of the River Dendre. Finally, on 13 July 1920, the 20th Hussars were serving with General Ironside's force on the Izmit Peninsula when they came up against an estimated 350 Turkish nationalists who were occupying the village of Gebze. The regiment took up a position east of the village, and a patrol under a Sergeant Waite of C Squadron charged three enemy snipers and sabred them. As the defenders retired from the village, a troop, also from C Squadron, under a Sergeant Mountford, mounted two further charges, cutting down seven more. According to the 20th Hussars' War Diary, the regiment lost one man wounded and one horse killed in the day's fighting. *Julian Humphrys*

We have heard much lately about the handful of surviving veterans of the First World War. How recently did the last surviving veteran of the Boer War die?

The last surviving veteran of the Boer War was George Frederick Ives, who volunteered in 1899 to serve in the Imperial Yeomanry after a succession of British defeats in South Africa stirred him into patriotic action. After the war ended he emigrated to Canada, where he lived for 90 years, finally dying in 1993 at the age of 111. *Nick Rennison*

CHAPTER 12

MONEY AND TRADE, OR THE RICHEST MAN WHO EVER LIVED

Have the British ever had to pay any taxes more ridiculous than William Pitt the Younger's notorious Window Tax?

I nominate the Bachelor Tax. For a brief period in 1695, William III's government taxed single men over the age of 25. It was on a sliding scale – a shilling for commoners up to £12, and 10 shillings for dukes. The late 17th and early 18th centuries were a golden age of odd taxes. In Russia Tsar Peter the Great famously taxed beards to encourage his subjects to adopt western European habits. In Britain William III taxed all sorts of things to finance war against Louis XIV. Some taxes, though, had other purposes; the Burial in Wool Act, for instance, which came into force in 1678, protected England's wool industry by taxing shrouds and coffin-linings made of anything except wool.

The Window Tax of 1696 was introduced to finance monetary reform partly masterminded by Sir Isaac Newton, though it later became part of the general revenue stream. The tax was modified in 1747 to introduce different rates according to the number of windows you had. It wasn't abolished until 1851. While it might appear ridiculous, the tax was rational, efficient and fair. Collectors could instantly see how much you owed (although some people tried to dodge it by bricking up windows), and, unlike the earlier Hearth Tax, which was still a bitter memory in the 1690s, collectors didn't enter people's homes. Like the modern Council Tax, it charged people according to the value of their property. Some critics called it a tax on light and fresh air, but most people didn't regard it as particularly crazy; it lasted over 150 years, after all. *Eugene Byrne*

Allowing for inflation, who's the richest person who ever lived?

Translating historic money values into modern terms is extremely problematic, and different cultures place different values on property, especially land. Many powerful rulers didn't always have much personal wealth, either because they were ascetic, or because they had to spend everything on maintaining their realms. The richest ruler who ever lived might be Tsar Nicholas II of Russia, with a personal fortune estimated at $290 billion in modern terms – much good it did him! We might find the winner is some 17th/18th/19th-century Indian prince or Chinese merchant. It could well be one of the great American plutocrats, such as Andrew Carnegie (OK, Scottish really), Henry Ford, Andrew Mellon or John D. Rockefeller. The American business magazine *Forbes* once reckoned that Rockefeller (1839–1937) was the wealthiest American ever. Bill Gates or Warren Buffet are strictly second division by comparison.

The richest Britons were probably aristocrats with large landholdings. *The Richest of the Rich: The Wealthiest 250 People in Britain Since 1066* by Philip Beresford (compiler of the *Sunday Times* Rich List) and William D. Rubinstein (Harriman House, 2007) reckons that the wealthiest man in English history was Alan Rufus (d. 1093), a Breton who accompanied William the Conqueror, with landholdings that would be worth over £80 billion now. *Eugene Byrne*

Which was the largest-ever tax bill?

Governments since before the dawn of history have demanded taxes, and most have been paid in the form of goods, such as a proportion of grain grown or livestock raised. Modern concepts of taxation rely on several things. A money economy is necessary, as is the existence of reasonably reliable accounts for businesses and individuals, and government accountants able to calculate tax totals. Lacking such things, taxation was usually levied either on a flat rate per head of population, or on the basis of moving trade goods that could be counted as they entered and left a town or state.

The earliest cash tax on income was introduced in the year 10 by the Chinese emperor Wang Mang. It could be levied only on professionals, who were obliged to keep financial books; peasants and nobles were exempt. In 1487 John Morton, Lord Chancellor of England, devised a novel method of calculating a nobleman's wealth for taxation purposes. He simply guessed, but justified his estimate based on the size of the nobleman's household. If he had a large household, he was obviously rich and could pay a large tax bill. If he had a small household, he was obviously saving money, in which case he could pay a large tax bill. Some noblemen were impoverished by what became known as 'Morton's Fork', and lost almost all their wealth.

In the modern world, tax bills for individuals are a matter of great secrecy between the person and the State, so it is impossible to be certain as to the largest tax bill ever paid by an individual person. However, corporate tax bills *are* made public, and the biggest paid by a business in any country at any time was around $30 billion – from the Exxon oil company to the US Treasury in 2007. The fine detail of the bill had not been computed at the time this book went to press, but it is unlikely to vary by more than $200 million or so. *Rupert Matthews*

Which was the cheapest British coronation?

No doubt some of the coronations held in early medieval times were carried out on a very limited budget, but the cheapest coronation of modern times was undoubtedly that of King William IV, held on 8 September 1831. William had come to the throne in June 1830 amid great controversy over the enormous bills run up by his extravagant predecessor, George IV, and in the midst of the bitter political disputes that would lead to the Great Reform Act of 1832. On both counts it was thought wise to dispense with the elaborate ceremonial and lavish entertainments that had graced George IV's coronation.

William himself detested formal public occasions. He suggested that there should be no separate coronation ceremony at all, arguing that he was going to be wearing his crown to dissolve Parliament and that he could take his coronation oath then. Traditionalists talked him out of that idea, but even so, the slimmed-down coronation cost a very modest £30,000. Many centuries-old traditions surrounding the coronation were ditched, never to reappear. The Royal Champion, for instance, did not ride fully armoured into the state banquet and challenge to fight to the death anyone who disputed William's right to reign. Indeed, there was no state banquet at all. *Rupert Matthews*

Which is the largest financial fraud in history?

The difficulty of accurately transposing historic monetary values into modern currencies makes comparison between modern and ancient frauds difficult. However, in terms of proportion of national wealth, one of the biggest frauds of past generations must be that perpetrated by the Scottish economist John Law in France. Law's basic idea was to abolish the existing inefficient systems of private monopolies and tax farming with a single, state-owned bank and state-owned commercial company. The French government in 1719 was saddled with huge debts of around 1.6 billion livres when its annual income was only around 150 million livres. After John Law outlined his plan he was appointed controller general of finances and went to work. He began in 1716 by founding the Banque Générale, which began issuing paper money backed by the government. Then, in 1717, he bought the Mississippi Company, which had the monopoly of trade to French colonies in North America. Law then began hyping up the value of the American trade and its potential for growth, which boosted the share prices in the Mississippi Company. In the spring of 1719 shares were worth 500 livres each, but the price rose rapidly to around 10,000 livres by February 1720, and 18,000 livres by June.

Meanwhile, Law had undertaken a complex series of trades that swapped government debt for equity in the company. New shares were issued to dilute the value of each share, and the new capital was used to purchase more government debt. By July 1720 all government debt had been offloaded to the Mississippi Company, which could afford the burden on the basis of the false prospectuses of future income put about by Law. In July 1720 a group of financiers who had warned against the scheme spoke out. Confidence in the venture collapsed and the share price fell steeply back to 500 livres. Effectively, investors in the company had lost their fortunes, while the government had offloaded its debt on to their accounts.

The resulting furore cost Law his job, as it did many government ministers who had been involved in the scheme. But nobody got their money back and the French government was free of debt. Many modern governments must wish that they could pull a similar trick to offload their accumulated debts. *Rupert Matthews*

Why is Edinburgh's main shopping thoroughfare called Princes Street? Which prince was it named after?

It refers to princes in the plural. Part of the New Town development of Edinburgh in the late 18th century, the street was named after the sons of George III. Earlier parts of the development were called George Street and Charlotte Square (after the king and his queen). *Nick Rennison*

Which is the oldest-known business still going?

So far as can be established, the oldest business that is still a going concern is a small family-run inn in Japan called the Houshi Ryokan. The business has certainly been run by 46 generations of the same family. There is less certainty about the precise year in which the inn was opened to the public, but it is usually stated to have begun trading in or close to the year 717.

According to legend handed down within the family, the inn owes its foundation to Taicho Daishi, one of the great Buddhist missionaries to Japan. In the early 8th century Taicho fell asleep on the slopes of the sacred mountain Hakusan and saw in a dream the sacred spirit of the mountain. This deity told him to travel to the village of Awazu, where he should dig at a certain spot to discover naturally hot springs of water with powerful medical properties. Taicho did as instructed and revealed the sacred springs. Before leaving to continue his missionary wanderings and spiritual studies, Taicho instructed his disciple Garyo Houshi to stay behind and tend the holy waters. Houshi cheerfully followed his master's orders. Within a short time the numbers of people coming to visit the sacred spring became so great that he opened a small inn to provide them with shelter and refreshment. This inn has developed over the centuries to become the Houshi Ryokan.

Today the inn comprises four buildings, the Shinshun no Yakata (early spring building), Haru no Yakata (spring building), Natsu no Yakata (summer building), and Aki no Yakata (autumn building). A wide range of traditional and wholesome foods is on offer to guests, while linked shops offer a number of local craftworks to visitors. *Rupert Matthews*

What did the ancients use as the working means of applying standard measures of length, weight and volume?

Almost as soon as people began to buy and sell things – grain, wine or land – there was a need for commonly accepted ways to measure these commodities. Unsurprisingly, each culture and civilisation in the ancient world came up with its own preferred measure, but most of them shared a common feature: the human body. The biblical cubit, for instance, was the distance from the elbow to the tip of the middle finger, about 17 inches (44 centimetres). The Roman mile, from the word for 'thousand', was the distance of 1000 paces. Weights were based on real objects that were readily to hand. The 2nd century BC measure for gold, the *gerah*, translates to metric at about 0.5 grams. It is thought to have originally been the equivalent of a grain of wheat. Foods tended to be measured by volume rather than weight, and these measures were more obscure.

The Middle Eastern *homer* was, in theory, the amount an ass could carry all day without trouble – about 50 gallons (200 litres).

With such a variety of measures in use, it is not surprising that dishonest merchants tried to cheat. The Bible (Proverbs 20:23) states that 'Divers weights are an abomination unto the Lord'. Many market towns had a set of 'official' weights and measures against which suspect traders could be forced to check their own equipment. *Rupert Matthews*

Have bank holidays anything to do with banks?

The concept of a bank holiday is unique to Britain and Ireland. Other countries do have mandatory days off work for the population, but these tend to be linked to either holy days or to government events. In the USA, for example, federal holidays are tied to dates in the government calendar, while in Italy public holidays are traditionally saints' days, which may vary from city to city.

Prior to the 19th century, Britain followed the more usual European custom of employers giving their workers certain days off during the year as dictated by custom. These were often saints' days, but could also include local holidays on which festivals or fairs traditionally took place. That changed when railways spread over the land, making long-distance travel and commerce much easier. It was suddenly inconvenient for a businessman to travel on business only to find that the town he was visiting had a holiday for a local parade. By the 1850s most businesses were abandoning their local, customary holidays and replacing them with the four holidays given by the Bank of England. These 'bank holidays' were 1 May, 1 November, Good Friday and Christmas Day. In most cases this involved workers having fewer days off work than before. Norwich, for example, had customarily had 15 holidays, so there was, unsurprisingly, some discontent.

In 1871 the government took a hand and introduced the Bank Holidays Act. This added several new public holidays: New Year's Day (in Scotland only), Easter Monday, Whit Monday, the first Monday in August and Boxing Day. A century later the government added the Bank of England's May Day holiday to the official list. In 1903 St Patrick's Day was added, but only for Ireland. Scotland gained St Andrew's Day in 2007. England and Wales do not yet have their patron saints' days as bank holidays, though there are campaigns to rectify this. *Rupert Matthews*

What was the first business school?

Until fairly recently most people did not go to school at all, never mind something as specialised as a business school. Those who wished to learn anything about business or trade would have gone to work with relatives in a family business, or applied to join a trades guild. The formalised training schemes offered by guilds were usually termed 'apprenticeships'. These could last for anything up to seven years and involved long hours of arduous training before final examinations took place and the guild masters judged the work of the apprentice to see if he was fit to open a business of his own.

The idea of having a separate institution to teach business methods did not emerge until the founding of the Aula do Comércio in Lisbon in 1759. This specialist school took in the sons of merchants after they had graduated from more basic schools that had taught them the skills of reading, writing, arithmetic, history and the like. The Aula taught the specific business skills of keeping financial books, understanding insurance and comprehending the often complex contracts that merchants had to sign. The school survived for almost a century before it closed its doors in 1844.

Meanwhile, something rather closer to the modern concept of a business school had opened in Paris in 1819 in the shape of the Ecole Supérieure de Commerce, now part of the ESCP–EAP European School of Management. The Ecole was not so narrowly focused as the Lisbon Aula, and covered a much wider range of business skills. Even so, the idea was slow to catch on. It was not until 1881 that the next business studies institution opened – in Pennsylvania. Thereafter a large number of business schools opened across the developed world. Britain's first such establishment was the Manchester Business School, now part of Manchester Metropolitan University, which opened in 1889. *Rupert Matthews*

Why does the tax year start on 6 April?

Until 1752, the financial year officially began on Lady Day, 25 March, one of the 'quarter days' when rent became due. In 1752 Britain changed from the Julian calendar to the Gregorian calendar, and 11 days were 'lost' as a result. Add these 11 days to the old Lady Day and you get a tax year beginning on 6 April.
Nick Rennison

Why do we talk about a 'baker's dozen' and why is it different from a normal dozen?

During the Middle Ages the price and weight of bread were very strictly regulated. In years of good harvests, bakers sold surplus bread to wholesalers, but the regulations meant that it was difficult for the wholesalers to make a profit unless the bakers put in an extra or 'vantage' loaf for each dozen sold. *Nick Rennison*

In the recent film *Flags of Our Fathers* it is claimed that the United States was in such financial difficulty in early 1945 that it might have to make peace with Japan. Is this true?

Joe Rosenthal's Pulitzer Prize-winning photograph of the raising of the US flag by six marines on Mount Suribachi, Iwo Jima, on 23 February 1945 was widely published in America, and used to launch the seventh war savings bond. Three of the marines, including the Pima Indian Ira Hayes, were used in the subsequent tour to sell the bonds. It was the most successful of the war bonds, and raised over $24 billion towards the war effort. However, the suggestion that this was necessary to continue the war is an overstatement. As the historian David Kennedy notes, 'Money for defence was no problem.' Instead 'the government's principal worry in wartime was not too little money but too much'. While war bonds contributed to financing the war, their main function was to control inflation. Taxation also increased in the US during the war, and paid 45 per cent of the overall war cost, which was in excess of $300 billion. The hyperbole used in Clint Eastwood's film reflected the need to sell the war rather than simply to raise money. This was a feature of all the war bond drives that were launched with the support of entertainers and movie stars, such as Bob Hope and Betty Grable, from 1941.

The bond campaigns avoided the almost hysterical and coercive methods adopted during the First World War, opting instead for a voluntary approach. By 1945 their function was to maintain morale and continue support for the war effort because although victory had been secured in Europe, the island-by-island campaign against Japan was incredibly bloody. Over a third of the 60,000 marines who landed on Iwo Jima were killed or wounded – among them three of those involved in the Mount Suribachi flag-raising. *Neil Wynn*

When was the first recorded instance of reducing the price of an article by a minute amount to make it appear cheaper?

For the greater part of shopping history items for sale did not have any price attached to them. Shoppers in Babylon, Carthage, Rome and Tudor London bargained and haggled with shopkeepers over the price of everything. So far as is known, the first shop to attach price tags to its goods was Peter & James Ferry, a silk merchant in London. In the autumn of 1744 the Ferry brothers announced a sale of silk for ladies' dresses. The poster they put up stated, 'The lowest price will be fixed on each piece, without any abatement.'

The first shop to use price tags for ordinary business is thought to have been Flint & Palmer on London Bridge. They introduced fixed price tags in 1750, and later pioneered the practice of taking cash only. Even the most exalted shopper had to pay in coin at the moment of purchase rather than having an account to be settled up later. The idea proved popular with country families who rarely came to London. By visiting a shop with fixed prices, they could be reasonably certain that they were not being cheated by a sharp trader.

By about 1800 most ready-made clothes and other items were sold with fixed prices, and although documentary evidence is lacking, it seems that promotional prices and reductions were being used by at least 1805. *Rupert Matthews*

What is the origin of the Cinque Ports, and which ports were they?

Cinque (pronounced 'sink') comes from the Norman-French word for 'five', and denotes a confederation of ports in southeast England. The original five, the 'head ports', were Hastings, New Romney, Hythe, Dover and Sandwich. The origin of the confederation goes back to Anglo-Saxon times (or earlier) and reflected the importance of these ports' trading links with the Continent. After the Norman Conquest they were required to supply ships and crews to the king for set periods, not only in wartime, but also to transport the king, his armies and members of his entourage to and from Normandy or elsewhere on the Continent. In return, the ports were accorded considerable autonomy and exemption from a lot of taxation, and could levy their own taxes and hold their own courts. Dignitaries from the Cinque Ports also had the right to carry the canopy over the monarch's head in the coronation procession. Nonetheless, the ports' duty of 'ship service' to the Crown was a heavy one, and the five head ports brought several neighbouring towns and villages into the arrangement in return for a share in the privileges. The most important of these were Rye and Winchelsea, which eventually gained equal status to the head ports. The Cinque Ports' commercial and military importance had become negligible by Tudor times, but many of their privileges lasted into the 19th century. *Eugene Byrne*

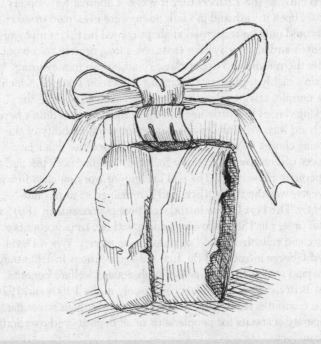

Did you know...?

In 1915, Stonehenge was bought as a birthday present for £6600. The Antrobus family, who had owned the monument since 1824, sold it to a businessman named Cecil Chubb, who wanted the monument for his wife. Reportedly, Mrs Chubb didn't much appreciate her birthday gift, and three years later her husband donated the stone circle to the nation. *Nick Rennison*

When was the first mail-order catalogue published?

The first mail-order catalogue was produced by New Jersey-born Aaron Montgomery Ward in 1872. It consisted of a one-page list of 162 items. Three years later the Montgomery Ward catalogue introduced the now-familiar phrase 'Satisfaction Guaranteed or Your Money Back' into retailing. *Nick Rennison*

How was money transferred around the country before banks were available for ordinary people?

As recently as the 19th century it was not unusual for workers to be paid both in cash and in kind. Some were even paid in tokens that could only be redeemed at shops owned by their employers, an unfair and abusive system that took a long time to stamp out. While the middle and upper classes could move money using Britain's highly sophisticated banking and credit systems, which, for example, saw people using banknotes instead of coin, the working classes had little need to move money – and didn't have much anyway. With the growing prosperity and mobility of the working classes in Victorian times, people used the financial services offered by the friendly societies, building societies and the cooperative movement. The real linchpin of working-class finance, however, was the Post Office, and it remained so until quite recently. The Post Office introduced savings accounts in 1861, and postal orders in 1881, allowing people without bank accounts a secure and reliable method of transferring money. When David Lloyd George introduced the first old-age pensions in 1909 they were paid at Post Offices, as were subsequent welfare benefits. Most Britons acquired bank accounts only in the 1960s and 1970s, when computer technology made it possible for high street banks to operate accounts for people with small deposits and overdrafts. *Eugene Byrne*

Why do we buy our goods from 'grocers' and 'greengrocers'? What is a 'grocer'?

A grocer was originally a wholesaler, somebody who bought goods in bulk. The word derives from the medieval Latin *grossus*, meaning 'big' or 'large'. In the 15th and 16th centuries grocer came to mean any trader in food, and the term was eventually applied to a small shopkeeper. *Nick Rennison*

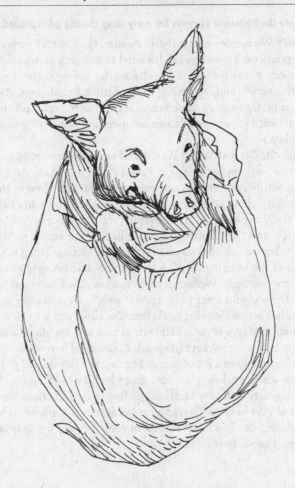

Why do we talk about buying a pig in a poke?

The phrase dates from the 16th century, recorded as 'When ye proffer the pigge, open the poke' in a list of advice to market traders. A poke was a sack in which goods for sale, such as a piglet, might be kept. The idea is that you should make sure you look in the poke and check that the pig is there before you part with your money. *Nick Rennison*

What are the historical reasons for early shop closing on Wednesday?

It wasn't Wednesday everywhere! Around the country early closing days on Thursdays are (or used to be) very common. In a few places it was Tuesday. Early closing day sprang up in Victorian times, and, according to the British Retail Consortium, this was partly to allow owners and staff time to replenish stocks and deal with paperwork. It also compensated for having to work at weekends.

Until the Second World War, it was common for Britons of all classes to work on Saturday mornings, if not the whole day, leaving Saturday afternoon and evening as the only time of the week when whole families could shop together. For many shops, particularly in cities, Saturday evening was the busiest time of the week, and they'd often stay open until quite late at night. Wednesday was an obvious choice for early closing, being in the middle of the working week. A town might choose an alternative day if, for example, Wednesday was market day. Shops and pubs in any town would want to be open if people were coming in from miles around looking to do business deals and a week's shopping. Friday was definitely out, as that was the day many workers had wage packets to spend. Likewise, Thursday was early closing day in a lot of places because the day before pay day was when working-class customers had the least money. Indeed, one reason why local and parliamentary elections are almost always held on Thursdays is because it is (or used to be) early closing day in a lot of places, making it easier for shop staff to vote. *Eugene Byrne*

CONTRIBUTORS

There are lots of people to thank for their contribution to this book, including *BBC History Magazine*'s readers (for providing such interesting questions), the researchers and the fact-checkers (past and present). Many have contributed to *BBC History Magazine* each month and, without them, this book would not be possible. Below are some short biographies about the current *BBC History Magazine* team and key contributors, whose names appear most frequently throughout the book. We would like to apologise should there be any errors or omissions from the below list.

Dave Musgrove has edited Britain's bestselling history monthly, *BBC History Magazine*, for several years. Prior to that, he edited *Living History Magazine*. He has a doctorate in medieval landscape archaeology, and is an expert on the wetland drainage strategies of the 12th-century monks of Glastonbury Abbey. He also maintains an interest in the implications for the prehistoric wetland archaeological record of the activity of *Castor fiber*, the European beaver.

Rob Attar is Features Editor of *BBC History Magazine*. He studied journalism and history at university, and has a particular interest in the Second World War and the Soviet Union. In his spare time he enjoys writing (but not reading) poetry. One day he would like to be able to divide his time between Bristol and the south of France.

Eugene Byrne is a freelance journalist and author specialising in history and heritage and heritage tourism. He has also written three science fiction novels, as well as a history of Bristol and biographies of Isambard Kingdom Brunel and Charles Darwin in comic form. He lives in Bristol and does all his own ironing.

Julian Humphrys is a writer, lecturer and broadcaster who loves to take an offbeat look at Britain's history. He is a regular contributor to *BBC History Magazine*'s 'Diversions' pages, and also compiles its 'Milestones' section of historical anniversaries, as well as all the top ten lists that also appear in this book. Julian spent several years on the staff of London's National Army Museum, and is the author of a number of books and articles on battles and sieges. He spends much of the summer leading groups around Britain's battlefields, castles and abbeys.

Rupert Matthews took to history at an early age, visiting Stonehenge, Avebury, West Kennet and other ancient monuments with his mother when he was still a toddler. Rupert entered publishing on leaving school, working at Reader's Digest, Hamlyn, Octopus and other publishers. Since taking up writing full time, Rupert has had over 100 books published on a variety of subjects, most of them history-related. He is married with one daughter.

Roger Moorhouse is a historian and author specialising in Nazi Germany and modern Central Europe. His most recent book was *Killing Hitler*, an account of the surprisingly numerous attempts on Hitler's life. A regular contributor to *BBC History Magazine* over the last decade, he is currently working on a book about civilian life in wartime Berlin, and is toying with the idea of writing a historical novel.

Nick Rennison is a writer, editor and regular contributor to *BBC History Magazine*. His books include *Sherlock Holmes: An Unauthorised Biography*, *Roget: The Man Who Became a Book* and *The Good Reading Guide*. He has a particular interest in Victorian social history, and is currently writing a crime novel set in the 1870s.

Professor Gary Sheffield holds the Chair of War Studies at the University of Birmingham. An expert in 20th-century military history, his many publications include *Douglas Haig: War Diaries and Letters 1914–18* (edited with John Bourne) and *Forgotten Victory: The First World War – Myths and Realities*. He is currently writing a book on the experience of the British soldier in the Second World War. He broadcasts on radio and television, and writes for the national press.

INDEX

abdication 129
abortion 12
accidents 20, 64
Acres, Birt 75
Act of Settlement 129
Adelin, William 15
advertising 157
Aelfeah 113
aerosol cans 159
Agent Orange 179
air raid shelters 176–7
Albert, Prince 115
Alen, John 113
Alexander of Greece 16
Alexander III of Scotland 19
Allenby, General 173
Alma-Tadema, Sir Lawrence 167
America 133, 172, 186–8, 209
American Civil War 179, 193
American Declaration of Independence 130
American flag 122
An-Nâsir, Muhammad 115
Anatomy Act 1832 141
Anderson, Sir John 176–7
Anderson, Mary 166
Andorra 126
Andrew, Prince 185
angels 107
animals 68, 160, 179
Anne of Great Britain 129
appeasement 38–9
Aquinas, St Thomas 107
archaeologists 57
Aristotle 62, 108
Armageddon 105, 111
Armistice 190–1, 196–7

Aryan race 127
Assizes 147
Assyrians 194
Astley's 46
astronauts 166
Atrebates 36
Attlee, Clement 177
Austen, Jane 46
Austin, Henry 'Bunny' 21
Australia 146, 158
Ayscough, James 163
Aztecs 161

Bach, J.S. 52
Bachelor Tax 201
Bacon, Delia 43
Bacon, Francis 43
Baddeley Cake 100
baker's dozen 209
Baldwin, Stanley 124
Balzac, Honoré de 48
bank holidays 207
Barbarossa, Frederick 15
Barclay, Captain 8, 75
Baret, Jeanne 168
Barlow, John Perry 52
Barnard, John Jervis 84–5
Barton, Elizabeth 153
Basevi, George 63
Baxter, Jeff 'Skunk' 52
bear-baiting 68–9
Beaton, David 113
Becket, Thomas 113
Beckjord, Suprabha 81
Bede, Venerable 19–20
Bedlam 150
beekeepers 62
beheading 141–2
Bell, Alexander Graham 167

Belzoni, Giovanni 57
Bentham, Jeremy 141
Berengaria 130
Beresford, Philip 202
Bergman, Ingrid 21
Berlioz, Hector 103
Bevan, Aneurin 32
Bible 44, 112, 207
Billy the Kid 143
birthday bumps 112–13
Bismarck (battleship) 182
Black Death 26–7
blacksmiths 63
Blackwell, Elizabeth 27
Blair, John Hunter 36
Bligh, Captain 124
blindness, in one eye 27
blood poisoning 16
Bloomer, Amelia 162
bloomers 162
Blue Lamp, The (1950) 140
Blue Peter (flag) 36–7
Boateng, Paul 133
Bock, Frederick 197
Bocksar (aircraft) 197
Boer War 199
Boleyn, Anne 15, 22–3, 52
Bonaparte, Charles-Joseph 147
Bono, Sonny 52
bootleggers 93
Botting, Eirene 150
Boudicca 14, 192
Bougainville, Louis Antoine de 168
bowls 85–7
Bradford, Dorothy 15
Bradley, Omar 68
Braine, John 53
Brandon, Frances 131

217

Index